Dominate!

The Digital Marketer's Step by Step Approach for the Ultimate Business Website

October 2014

DOUG WILLIAMS

Copyright 2014 by Williams Business Services, Inc.

Published by Williams Business Services, Inc.

Graphics and Cover Design by- Doug Williams
Edited by- Theresa Potratz

All rights reserved. No part of this book may be used, reproduced, distributed, or transmitted in any manner without prior written permission except in the case of brief quotations embodied in critical reviews and articles.

First Edition October 2014

Table of Contents

Contents

Forward 5
About the Author 15
1. Start With the "Why" 17
2. What Do They Want? 27
3 Image and Branding 39
4 Closing the Deal 51
5 Size-up Your Competition 71
6 Create Your Website Plan 83
7 Crafting Your Message 97
8 You Must Design For Mobile 111
9 Getting Your Website Built 121
10 Traffic Strategies 101 133
11 Metrics and KPIs 151
12 After Your Site Goes Live 165
Website Planning Checklist 179
References and Sources 182
Index 185

Forward

By Doug Williams

The World Wide Web has been around for 25 years. In December of 1992 the entire Internet was made up of just 50 websites[1]. By 2014 this number has grown to 1 billion websites[2].

Searches by consumers and websites by businesses have made an effective business website a requirement for companies marketing their goods and services. For small businesses, digital marketing (this used to be called Internet marketing) is the primary marketing expense.

Ten years ago it was easy to launch a website and optimize a website to attract traffic. Today the landscape is far more competitive and Google has made it much harder to manipulate the search results.

This is a book about how to plan your website using the methods and systems that I use with my clients. We will go through the steps on how to properly plan and market your business on the web in a step by step process.

You will plan a website that will market to your best buyers. It is not about the technology of building a website. It is marketing strategy and techniques that will transform your website into a lead generator… an email list builder or an online sales machine.

The problem with most websites

Ever notice that as you search the web using Google (or any search engine) that what comes up is low quality and doesn't help you with the problem you are trying to solve?

You go from site to site looking around for 2-10 seconds. When you don't see what you are looking for, you hit the back button and go onto the next search result.

Every now and then you find something interesting. You look around and go deeper into the website. You mentally tell yourself that this could be the answer.

Trying to be thorough, you keep on looking. After 10 minutes or so you realize that that what you found at the beginning was the best solution. Now you can't seem to remember what site that was?

If only you had thought to bookmark that page… or signed up for that free eBook. Oh well… you will come back and search again when you have more time. Having enough time is the real issue.

Challenge #1 Internet marketing is pull type marketing

Traditional marketing is "push" type marketing. You craft your message and deliver it to your target audience. This is how radio, TV, newspaper, magazine and direct mail advertising works. It is the same for building signage, billboard advertising, vehicle signage and even tradeshow booths.

It is just like fishing in which you create irresistible bait and wait for a "bite." You create an enticing advertising piece and wait for a prospective customer to wander by.

Traditional advertising is an active form of marketing. You are the hunter and your prospect is the prey. You broadcast or push out your message and wait for a response.

Internet marketing is "pull" type marketing. Your prospects are searching for you. People have a problem or something they want to buy and they sit down at their computer or get on their mobile phone and search on Google. They are actively searching to find you.

In pull marketing, your customer is in control. They are the hunter. They use search engines to find a solution to a specific need or problem that they have. You need to make your website easy and appealing to find. You need to design logical selling sequences or trails for visitors to follow.

Pull Marketing Attracts

Figure F.1 Pull Marketing

To be successful in Internet marketing you need to clearly understand the psychology behind how people search. You need to know how to make your site visible when people are searching for what you sell.

When they arrive to your website you need to clearly give them what they are searching for and then allow them to take immediate action.

You need to understand the buying cycle for your product or service. Some products have a very short almost "instant" buying cycle. This applies to many B2C (business-to-consumer) products where your goal is to provide instant gratification with ultra-fast delivery.

B2B or business-to-business has a long often many step sales process. This applies to many business services. Here you often use a request a quote form or get them to sign-up for your email list with a free eBook or free report.

The important thing to do is to plan how to connect with your best buyer and to storyboard out your initial interaction with them.

Challenge #2 The Internet is huge, where do you start?

The enormity of the Internet creates a challenge and at the same time it creates a tremendous opportunity.

In 22 years the Internet grew from 50 websites to over 1 billion websites worldwide.[2]

Search is how people access information. In the US there are 245,203,319 Internet users which are 78.1% of the total population[3]. In March 2014, US Internet users performed 19 billion searches[4]. This translates into 79 searches per month for the average Internet user.

Instead of thinking of the Internet as a huge mass of people; you need to break it up into small segments or markets. You need to clearly profile your best buyer. Your best buyer is one or more buyer profiles that are most likely to buy what you are selling.

Let's say you have a business that advertises apartment rentals across the United States. It wouldn't do any good to be ranked #1 for the search term "apartments for rent." That is just not how people search for apartments.

People search for local apartments. Instead you would want to be found for "apartments for rent Northridge CA" or whichever area is local to your buyer.

This is an example of understanding your buyer.

Each geographic region is different and unique. As an example, let's look at different individual US states.

State or territory	% Population Online	Internet Users per Sq. Mile
Alabama	65%	59
Alaska	84%	1
California	80%	182
Mississippi	60%	37
Montana	73%	5
New Hampshire	92%	129
New Jersey	88%	886
Utah	89%	29
Washington DC	77%	6,782
US Averages	78%	63

Internet usage by US state or territory[5]

Alaska has the lowest density of Internet users per square mile, yet a high percentage of the population is online. This makes them an ideal candidate for web and email marketing. Washington DC has the highest density per square mile making it ideal for a combined Internet marketing combined with local traditional marketing such as radio or direct mail.

The Internet is filled with statistics and measurements that will help you develop strategies for your market. You need to focus your marketing efforts on specific segments. The more you focus, the better the results you will get.

Challenge #3 People are shifting to Mobile

There has been an explosive growth of smartphones and tablets causing a drop in desktop search and a big increase in mobile search.

Users of smartphones and tablets behave very differently[6]. In Q3 of 2012 ten percent of ecommerce spending came from primarily from tablets. Smartphones are used more on the go and are used for finding stores and checking prices prior to making a purchase. Tablets are used more for checking reviews and doing more in depth research.

Tablets are used much like a desktop PC with the primary activity being search while smartphones are used more for social.

Desktop PCs, tablets and smartphones are all very different channels with different uses. This needs to be factored into your website strategy.

Challenge #4 Website Visitors Arrive to the Website and Leave Quickly

It's amazing how fast website visitors size up a page. There have been lots of studies that have measured this. It really comes down to poorly created or irrelevant pages that get the "back" button in 2-10 seconds. A very interesting page may get up to 2 minutes of attention.

With the web, you need to communicate your value proposition within 10 seconds or less. Your website must be clearly organized, communicate your message AND give them a specific action to take.

If someone visits your website and then just leaves without taking action, then what benefit did you receive from their visit?

This would be like having a shop in the busiest mall in your town. You have a flood of people visiting, but no one buys. No one even slows down to ask a question. You would need to ask yourself "What's wrong?"

You need to design a clear and intuitive action into every page. You need to guide them to the next step in your selling sequence. You need to provide an easy and clear way to buy or request more information on every page.

Getting visitor traffic is only half the battle. Conversion of these people into buyers or at least adding them to your email list is an important priority. In this book we will present some powerful conversion strategies that will help turn your website traffic into revenue.

Grab a cup of coffee while you learn what it takes to create your own high impact website that will truly transform your business.

At the end of each chapter you will find the website planning checklist items discussed in that chapter. A complete website planning checklist can be found near the end of the book.

———————

Chapter Summary

This book is written as a guide for planning your business website. The focus is on strategies and techniques for creating a high performance website that will make a huge impact on your business. We will address and provide techniques for the key challenges that you face.

1. Internet marketing is different than traditional marketing. It is "pull" type marketing. Your prospect searches for you, rather than you broadcasting your message to them.

2. The Internet as a whole is huge; you need to focus your marketing efforts on specific segments. The more you focus on a niche, the more business you will get.

3. Mobile is the new growth frontier. People search and use their mobile smartphones and tablets very differently than desktop PCs.

Getting visitor traffic to your website is only half the battle. Conversion of these people into buyers or at least adding them to your email list is an important priority.

About the Author

Doug Williams

Doug Williams is president of Doug Williams Digital Marketing. He has started, grown and sold businesses, including a web development business. He has over 35 years of senior management experience, served on boards of directors and been a successful business consultant.

Doug Williams has been providing SEO and website planning services since 2002. What began as SEO for his own business consulting practice quickly grew into a SEO business. Then it grew into a 15 person Internet marketing business providing SEO services, website design and Internet marketing consulting.

In 2002, Doug Williams founded Doug Williams and Associates (DWA); a Website marketing company / Website building business with its core mission to help businesses grow. Doug has worked with many industry leaders to provide Internet marketing services to their clients.

In 2010 Doug sold his website marketing business to a larger website company that focused on producing high quality websites to major businesses.

In 2013 Doug started Doug Williams Digital Marketing which is a boutique digital marketing agency that provides premium quality digital marketing strategy consulting and premium websites to a small group of clients.

Prior to becoming a consultant, Doug spent much of his career in management, 22 of these years in senior management positions across a wide range of industries. During this time, Doug defined and put in place many key business systems and improvement strategies to create profitable operations.

In 2008, Doug published his first book Biz Blog Marketing. In 2010, Website Marketing Mastery was released. 2011 Mastering Blog marketing was released for Kindle and Nook eBook readers. In 2012, the eBook SEO Made Easy was published.

Doug has an MBA from Pepperdine University.

1. Start With the "Why"

You have made the decision that you need a new website. Start by looking at <u>why</u> you made that decision. This is the "why" that we are talking about.

Usually this starts with an emotional reaction to your present website. You could be ashamed of the image it portrays of your business. You could be disgusted at the lack of leads your site produced. You may be stressed by missing your business's financial goals.

Whatever your "why" is, use it to shape the objectives and the results you want from your new website. Never lose sight of your motivation for creating the new website. If your website fails to address the "why," you will never be happy with it.

Once you have made the decision to replace or even create your first website, you need to start building a list of some rational, logical results that you want this new website to produce for your company.

Set goals and measurable objectives for this new website. In chapter 11 we will discuss establishing metrics and key performance indicators so you can measure results.

Websites Should Deliver Results

Why should your business invest in a new website? The website should help you reach your business goals. A website should be planned to get specific results that will transform and grow your business by encouraging your best buyers to come and take specific actions.

4 Key Factors

1. **Website purpose**- This is your business objective such as to generate leads, book online sales, build your email list, etc. Your website needs to have a single primary purpose.

2. **Buyer profile**- A clear understanding of your best buyer, their motivations, their buying triggers and their buying process.

3. **Conversion**- Your site needs to present a credible image for business, your message needs to be clear and answer the problem visitors came to solve and you need get them to take action.

4. **Traffic**- Your best results come from people already searching for what you sell. You need a steady flow of qualified prospects that you can sell to.

Building good website plan is much like building a business plan. Your website should be treated like a stand-alone business unit. The more effort you put into a formal plan with strategies and tactics, the more likely you will be to succeed.

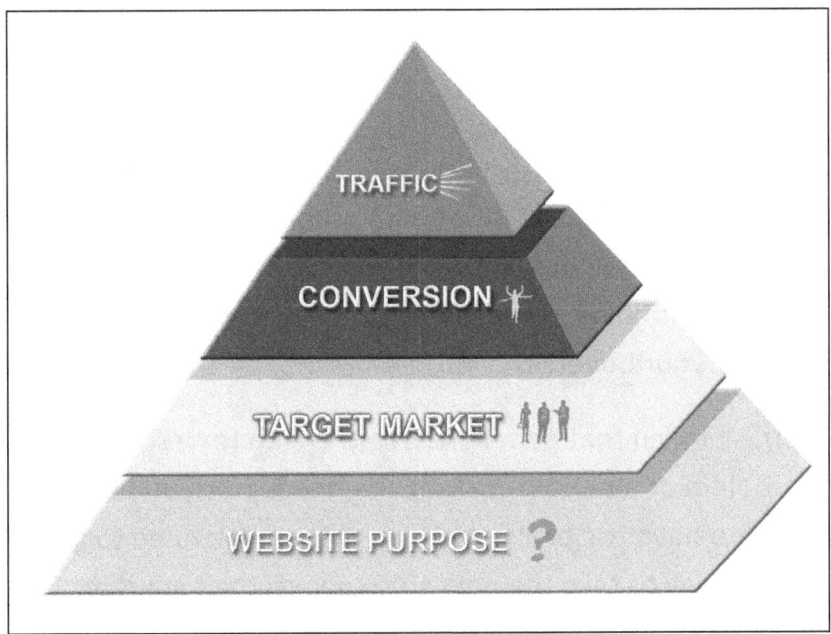

Figure 1.1 the Website Planning Pyramid

You will focus on getting visitors to take action. You are after only one thing: conversions. These can be getting visitors to fill out a form, make a purchase or even make a phone call. These conversions are really more about psychology than anything else.

You will notice that I refer to the people coming to your website not as visitors, but as your best buyers. You don't just want to attract just anybody that might be interested in what you sell. You want to focus on bringing people that are extremely interested. You want to attract people that have a current need. You want to attract people that will buy the best that you have and that will buy from you often.

The process of creating a great website is simple and straight forward. It is really about creating alignment with what you want your website to accomplish and the needs of your best buyer. Your site needs to provide the solution path for your buyer.

By this I mean that people search the web for a solution to a problem or a need. Your website needs to clearly show why you have the best solution and then you need to give them a way to take the next step toward their solution.

To really have an impact on your business, your website must attract your best buyers. You need to have a clear traffic strategy. You should develop multiple channels that will send buyers your way.

Traffic can come from organic Search Engine Optimization (SEO), paid search engine ads such as Google AdWords, social media and traditional marketing methods such as radio, TV and direct mail.

Website Purpose

Before you build your website, you need to ask yourself "Why I am building this website? What is the business reason for this site to exist? What is your website meant to do?" Here are 7 common purposes for a website.

1. Share information
2. Generate leads
3. Sell products online
4. Promote your brand
5. Interact with your customers
6. Build your email list
7. Recruit new staff

Before you start planning how you will approach your buyer, you need to understand what you want your website to do for you. What is <u>your</u> primary motive for creating your website?

The objective is not to generate traffic. It should not be a brochure that describes your business. For your website to have an impact on your business, you need to expect certain results from it. If you don't set goals, you can't achieve them.

If you are a non-profit, your primary objective might be fund raising or recruiting volunteers. If you are a government agency, you may want to publish information on applying for government grants or online lookup of information. If you are a medical office you may want to book appointments, or provide your location and hours of operation.

You need to take inventory of your business assets and strengths that you want to build on. Look at your Unique Selling Proposition (USP). What advantages do you have over your competition? What benefits will people have in doing business with you? Remember that people make buying decisions based on the differences, not how you are the same as your competition.

Once you have a clear laser like focus on what your website should do, then you can build your strategies to get these results. You want to focus your entire website around achieving the business results you want from your website.

Objectives for your website will be the specific results that you need. If your purpose is to generate leads, then you can set objectives around the number of quote requests or phone calls that your website is expected to generate. You will need to setup metrics to measure progress. For more information on selecting KPIs and metrics see chapter 11.

Buyer Profile

The most important thing you can do to increase your conversion rate is to have a deep understanding of your customer. You want a deep understanding of who they are and what is their motivation for buying?

As you build up your buyer profiles, ask yourself these questions.

1. Who are your best buyers? What do you know about them?

2. Why would they come? What are their motivations?

3. What makes them buy? What is the trigger that will cause them to buy?

Your website can be designed to address your best buyer persona on your home page. You can construct multiple selling sequences for your other buyer personas. You will likely develop your messaging on your website to encourage your best buyer and perhaps discourage those you do not want to target.

Your website needs to connect with your buyer. This comes from a deep understanding. It comes from using a shared language, a shared vocabulary, imagery, symbols and behavior. Content on your site needs to be both useful and aligned with the needs of your visitors. For more on understanding your buyer, see Chapter 2

Get Visitors to Take Action

Your website needs to be designed to be a conversion engine. The more focused your website is toward a single purpose, the better your results. The more possible actions a visitor to your website can take, the lower your conversion rate.

What affects conversion rates?

- Your design should instill confidence and trust.
- Use simple intuitive menus and navigation.
- Create Headlines and sub-headlines to tell your story.
- Your web page content should be benefit focused.
- Your content should flow like a well-orchestrated story.
- Solve your buyer's problem.
- Communicate your message and support your page headlines with compelling pictures or graphics.
- Use videos to educate and visualize products.
- Provide a clear and visible action for visitors to take.
- Your website should look trustworthy.

For more on conversion optimization see Chapter 4.

Traffic

Your website should be designed to attract prospects from Google search. Do this by doing keyword research and then building these keywords into your website's content.

Develop multiple traffic strategies such as social media and PPC advertising. For more on traffic strategies see Chapter 10.

Chapter Summary

Start by looking at why you are motivated to build this new website. Don't lose sight of this as you plan and build it. If you don't answer this why, you will never be happy with the new website.

Effective websites are designed for maximum impact on your business. In other words, they get results. There are 4 key components that make up the impact pyramid which is our model for producing high impact websites.

1. **Website purpose**- This is your business objective such as generate leads, direct online sales, build your email list, etc. Your website needs to have a single primary purpose.
2. **Buyer profile**- A clear understanding of your best buyer, their motivations, their buying triggers and their buying process.

3. **Conversion**- Your site needs to present a credible image for business, your message needs to be clear and answer the problem visitors came to solve and you need get them to take action.

4. **Traffic**- Your best results come from people already searching for what you sell. You need a steady flow of qualified prospects that you can sell to.

Website Planning Steps

☐ Describe why you want this new website

☐ What are your business marketing objectives

☐ Describe purpose and objectives for website

2. What Do They Want?

When a visitor comes to your website, what do they want? Why did they come?

This really is a study in psychology. You need to understand what your buyers are seeking, what they are thinking, what their motivations are and what their buying triggers are. In this chapter we will discuss the concept of your best buyer, developing a profile for your buyer and ways to get insight into what your visitors are searching for.

Some will come looking for information; some will arrive ready to buy. People seeking information may become buyers once they get enough information. Buyers will want to know why what you offer is different, why it is better.

Your website may have several different types of buyers. Each buyer will likely have different buying criteria. Here are 4 types of buyers.

1. **Price buyer-** They make their decision based on price and is bargain hunters. They treat products as commodities and put little emphasis on the quality of the solution.
2. **Features buyer-** They want state of the art products with the latest features. They will have a clearly defined need that a product feature will solve.

3. **Solutions buyer**- They are searching for a solution to a critical business issue such as increasing revenue or profitability for a business. Consumers may be looking for retirement security.
4. **Custom buyer**- They want a customized solution that is tailored to their situation. They avoid stock solutions and they rely on the seller's skills to develop a unique solution for them.

Best Buyers

What separates an average website from a top converting site? It is focusing on the needs of your best buyer. Your best buyers are the most interested and most likely to buy your product or service. They are the easiest to convert from first time lookers into repeat buyers.

Who are your best buyers? What do you know about them? How old are they? How well educated? What do you know about their income level? Do they live or work in a particular area? Are they from a particular industry? What job position do they hold?

Why would they come to your website? What are their motivations? What personal desires are they trying to satisfy? What are the things that bother them or their pain points? Are you closely matching their needs with what you have to offer?

What makes them willing to buy? What is the trigger that will cause them to buy? By showing that you clearly understand their pain, people become much more open to buying. You want to present a website that clearly solves their issue.

You will likely construct profiles or personas for your buyers. A Buyer Persona is a fictitious, specific and concrete representation of your targeted website visitors. This is a way to put a personal, human face on a group of visitors that are seeking certain goals.

Your website can be designed to address your best buyer persona on your home page. You can construct multiple selling sequences for your other buyer personas. You will likely develop your messaging on your website to encourage your best buyer and perhaps discourage those you do not want to target.

As an example a staffing services website will have two distinct groups of people they market to. There are businesses hiring managers that need to find employees and people that are seeking jobs. Each has very different needs and each requires a different selling sequence with a different call to action.

Your website needs to connect with your buyer. A great connection comes from good communication. Good communication isn't talking; it comes from a deep understanding. It comes from using a shared language, a shared vocabulary, imagery, symbols and behavior. Content on your site needs to be both useful and aligned with the needs of your visitors.

Examples of Buyer Personas

Let's assume you have a business consulting website, these are two user personas that you might create.

Dave Johnson is a 38 year old long haul trucker that wants to start-up his own freight hauling business. With two years college education and 15 years behind the wheel of an 18 wheeler, Dave has learned the ins and outs of the freight hauling industry. Dave and his driving partner (and wife) Sally are looking for help in forming their own company and how to best market their services.

John Mavor is a 32 year old personal trainer with a loyal following of clients. John has a four year degree in Physical Fitness and Wellness and 8 years in operating his own business. Located in the Washington DC area, John wants to take his business to the next level by opening up his own facility. He is looking for a business coach to guide him through the process.

Both John and Dave may be of a similar age and gender, but they have very different needs. One wants to launch a new business, the other to grow an existing business in two very different service industries. Two different navigation paths could be designed to improve website conversion. Different tools, reports and resources can be offered for these two conversion paths.

What kinds of things should you include in a buyer persona?

1. Background- name and nickname, photo, age, gender, education level and work experience.
2. Describe the individual- personality, timid or bold, communication style, computer skills.
3. Problem identification- what your visitor is seeking, what is the purpose, what are their expectations, goals and what is the problem to be solved?
4. Motivation level- urgency, desires, price vs. quality.

Psychology of Search

When people search on a search engine, what do they search for? Generally speaking, people search with a definite purpose. They have a question to be answered, information to research or something to buy.

Search engines are a tool for people to access information.

What are people searching for? It is whatever is impacting their life at that moment. They could be searching for a plumber to replace the hot water heater, to look at the menu of a local restaurant or how to make their lawn greener.

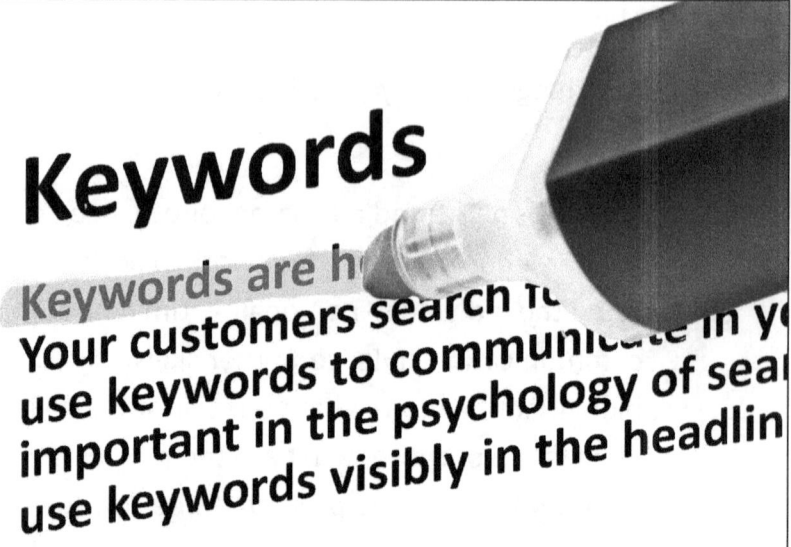

Figure 2.1 Keywords

Using Keyword Research

As a marketer, we look at usage patterns of how people search for specific products or services. We look at past searches to predict how people will search in the future.

Let's look at how people may look for a plumber. We start by looking at all plumbing related searches. We categorized all these phrases to look for patterns.

1. Fixtures- 54.3% of searches were for fixtures (kitchen sinks, faucets, bathroom fixtures)
2. Plumber- 19.1% of searches were for a plumber (plumber, plumbing contractor)

3. Parts- 16.3% were for parts (plumbing supplies, plumbing parts)
4. Problem- 10.3% of searches were for an urgent problem (broken pipe, toilet repair)

Phrases related to fixtures and parts would be more suited to a plumbing products store that sells to do-it-yourselfers. People most often search for a plumber using the word plumber, usually along with a city name. They also search frequently based on the nature of the problem.

This would mean a plumber's website should not only be optimized for "plumber + city" but also for the types of problems he solves or installations he does.

Keywords used in optimizing your website are linked to buyer psychology and conversion strategies. Search phrases give a view into what a searcher is thinking.

Buyer Phrases

You want to identify buyer keywords. These are phrases that show intent to take action. These are different than information seeking phrases. Simply focusing on attracting visitors that are motivated buyers will improve your website's conversion rate.

Example: If someone searches for "website optimization" they are likely seeking information about the SEO process. People searching for "website optimization services" or "website optimization Denver" are likely looking to buy services.

Local Intent: Including a city or other geographic reference indicates buyers that are searching for local businesses.

Phrase Length: People begin their buying process in the research phase with short 1-2 word keyword phrases. They are searching for more general phrases. As they get closer to making a buying decision, the search phrases become longer and more specific. They will include make, model or geographic location. Buyer keywords are typically 3-5 words or even longer.

Customer Words: You will want to think like your customer, not an industry expert. Did you know most realtors instinctively want to be found for "real estate for sale" yet most people actually search for "homes for sale"?

Focused Content: Focus your website on solving a narrow set of problems. This will be more attractive to someone seeking a solution provider. Specialists are more trusted than generalists.

We find that keyword research done at a very early phase of the project gives great insight into the problems people are trying to solve and helps develop buyer profiles. These same keywords help develop messaging across the website and to develop a content plan. Keyword research also helps in developing the SEO plan.

The best way is to do preliminary keyword research and then go back and select the most relevant phases to your business. We typically identify 100 phrases for a project and narrow this to 25 phrases based on relevance.

Keyword Selection Criteria

1. Relevance- Select keywords first based on relevance. Are they looking for what you provide?

2. Buyer Phrases- Look for phrases that indicate visitors are ready to take action.

3. Search Volume- Once you have narrowed your list of relevant buyer phrases, then choose based on the highest search volumes.

Keyword Research Tools

There are free and paid keyword research tools. Some do a better job or are faster to use. All work by querying search engines such as Google for their information. Google offers its own free keyword tool.

1. Google keyword planner (Free)
   https://adwords.google.com/KeywordPlanner

2. Wordtracker (Free)
   https://freekeywords.wordtracker.com

3. Wordtracker (Paid)
   http://www.wordtracker.com/

4. Market Samurai (Paid)
   http://www.noblesamurai.com/products.php

Chapter Summary

You need to understand what your buyers are seeking, what they are thinking, what their motivations are and what their buying triggers are.

You need to create a buyer profile or persona. This is a fictitious, specific and concrete representation of your targeted website visitors. This is a way to put a personal, human face on a group of visitors that are seeking certain goals.

Best buyers are the most interested and most likely to buy your product or service. They are the easiest to convert from first time lookers into repeat buyers.

Keyword research gives great insight into the problems people are trying to solve and helps develop buyer profiles. These same keywords help develop messaging across the website and to develop a content plan. Keyword research also helps in developing the SEO plan.

Website Planning Steps

- ☐ Describe your best buyer
- ☐ Develop buyer profiles or personas
- ☐ Do keyword research and rate for relevance

3 Image and Branding

How important is the "look" of your website? Your website is a reflection of your branding. It is how people see and judge your business.

According to the findings from the Stanford Web Credibility Project, 75% of web users admit making judgments about the credibility of an organization based on the design of its web site.[6]

Would you buy a new Rolex for $25 from a stranger? ...probably not. The price may be enticing, but you wouldn't trust that it was real. People do judge your business by its cover.

Your digital branding is more than just how your website looks. It is the sum of all the online perceptions, memories and experiences that people have of your products or company. Your digital branding strategy is more than making your brand memorable; it is about creating a connection and an expectation that you provide the best solution.

Difference between Branding and Marketing

Branding is about creating the unique name, image, story, expectations and values. Traditional marketing strategies are telling people why they should buy. Branding is the emotional arm of marketing. Branding is more strategic while sales and marketing is more tactical. Successful branding is emotional and creates customer loyalty.

 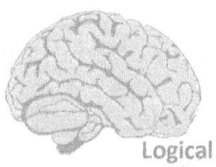

Emotional   Logical

BRANDING vs. **MARKETING**

Qualitative, Art, Logo, Colors, Design, Identity, Intangible, Motivates, Promises, Symbol, Communicates, Awareness, Trademarks, Shapes, Trust

Science, Quantitative, Target, Segmentation, Market Study, Advertising, Promotion, Pricing, Channels, Positioning, Advertising, Research, SEO

Figure 3.1 Branding vs. Marketing

6 Digital Branding Strategy Elements

1. Targeting- The message is carefully developed to reach the right audience. Your solution should create a high interest and appeal to this segment. You should have a clear understanding of their needs and wants. Conduct market analysis and surveys to gather data.

2. Logo- The logo is the single most important visual representation of your company's brand identity. A good logo is memorable, unique and simple; it conveys a message to your target audience. Use of taglines in logos is diminishing because they tend to be too limiting.
3. Domain- Memorable and easy to remember domain names are very important to the website brand identity. Google.com and target.com are examples of simple prominent brands where the domain matches their brand.

 *Try and use .COM to appear as a market leader since 76% of all domains in the US are .COM.*

4. Personality- This includes voice, message, style and design. There needs to be a consistent brand personality used in all communication. It is the brand personality that engages and interacts with your targeted audience. The voice and messaging used in copywriting can range from formal and highly technical to friendly and inviting.
5. Visibility- Create strategies to boost your brand's visibility to your target audience. Visibility strategies can include SEO, social media marketing, PR, online and offline advertising and promotional giveaways. Use of multiple channels increases effectiveness.
6. Consistency- Be consistent in your use of logo, colors and even how you present your company name. All

websites, emails, letterhead, etc. should use consistent branding.

A successful digital branding strategy creates an emotional connection with your prospective and current customers. It helps attract and retain loyal customers. Branding establishes a premium value that people are willing to pay more for.

What makes a good logo?

Your logo is a visual icon of your branding. You use your logo on your website, business cards, letterhead, brochures and in your email. A great logo is memorable, creates a visual impact and helps your company become easily remembered.

So, what makes a great logo? It is simple, distinctive, represents the company and has the illusion of action.

1. Simple means that it is not overly complex, can be reduced to a small size on a business card and doesn't have many complex and competing elements. Simple also means good contrast and a bold look.
2. Distinctive means being unique and memorable, graphic (not just letters), not being cluttered in look and something that has a unique look. The colors, shape and font should be used in combination to help the business stand out and not blend in.

3. Relevant- Your logo design should symbolize your business and create a positive first impression. Concentrate on an abstract image to represent the feel of your company's business. Shapes, curves and symmetry can convey meaning.
4. Illusion of action means the logo has the appearance of motion and doesn't just sit there. This draws in your visitor's attention. By adding in the image of a partially turned key, shapes or textures a logo can be made to show action. Think of the Nike Swoosh to illustrate running shoes.
5. Color and Contrast- A great logo must be easily seen and attract attention. Your choice of colors communicates emotion and is an important part of your message. Contrast can be created using colors, texture and use of white space.

A simple great logo may not be easy or quick to create, but it is powerful in your company's branding for marketing strategies or Internet marketing.

 *Need a new logo at a reasonable price? Use 99designs.com. For $300 you will get multiple designers competing and submitting logo designs.*

Selecting a Domain Name

Selecting a domain name is as much about branding as is creating a logo for your business. Your domain should be memorable, recognizable and easy to type out.

1. **Name Recognition-** In most cases the domain name should match the company name. This may mean the full company name (wellsfargo.com, or bestbuy.com) or using a recognizable abbreviation such as IBM.com or HP.com. You can also choose a keyword driven domain like GiftBaskets.com which is owned by Hayneedle Inc.
2. **Choose a .COM-** People naturally think first of a .COM before a .NET, .INFO or .BIZ. That is because in the US, 76% of all domains registered are .COM. If you use something other than a .COM, it forces you to emphasize the end (.NET or .BIZ) of your domain instead of the name itself when marketing. This hurts your branding strategy.
3. **Keep it Short-** This makes it easier to type. Don't sacrifice making it memorable though. Later I will tell you how. I made this mistake when I formed my company.
4. **Easy to Type-** Avoid the use of hyphens because people will forget to type them in. If your domain purpose is strictly for SEO, hyphens are fine. Including numbers makes your domain harder to type. Easy to remember should outweigh easy to type.
5. **Older Domains-** Buying existing domains can be a good idea. Search for domains that have had a website for several years and have a good number of inbound links. This can be an effective way of getting

a jump start on instant search engine rankings. You will pay extra, but this can be money as well.
6. Check Copyright- Avoid copyright infringement by checking copyright.gov. Your domain name should be relevant to your business name or business model (products, services) to be defensible against infringement.
7. Check History- Use the Wayback Machine www.archive.org to see what other site may have been on that domain. Sometimes these past sites may cause a problem for your future website. We had one client that purchased a short domain name for a children's motivational site only to later discover that the site once was home to a porn website. OUCH!

It is very important to choose the right domain name. Let me use my own company as an example.

In 2002 I started up my business as a consulting company and selected Doug Williams and Associates as my business name. Once my company name was established, I went searching for a suitable domain. The obvious one "DougWilliams.com" was taken. I knew shorter domain names were better, so I abbreviated my company name to "DWAssoc.com." Seems logical doesn't It?

This was a big mistake. Even though I did some things right – it was short, represented the company and was a .COM –

I overlooked a few important details. It wasn't memorable and people couldn't remember what it stood for; every time someone asked me for my email address, I found myself repeating the spelling three or four times. The domain wouldn't stick in their memory and didn't strengthen my brand.

I finally went out and purchased "DougWilliams.com" and paid a premium price for it. This was the best decision I could have made. Even though it was longer, it was memorable and reinforced my brand. Now, I never have to repeat the spelling of my email address to anyone.

Get your own domain and send email using that domain and avoid using Gmail, Hotmail, AOL or Comcast emails. These are fine for personal email, but for business you want to appear more stable, reliable, and professional. It's best to use yourname @yourcompany.com.

Choice of Color in Branding

Color is another powerful communicator that you can use in branding and should not be taken for granted. It can trigger emotional responses based on nationality, past experiences, and even personal preference. There have been numerous studies done on how different colors affect the majority of online visitors. In general, red, orange, and yellow are exciting colors while purple, blue and green are calming ones.

Below are example colors and what they tend to convey:

- Black: Elegance, formality, mystery, death and style.
- Blue: Stability, truth, professionalism, dignity, trust, peace and coolness.
- Brown: Endurance, casual, earthy, poverty and tradition.
- Copper: Professional growth, business productivity and money goals.
- Gold: Expensive, prestige, wisdom, attainment, high quality.
- Gray: Conservatism, seriousness and enhances messages of other colors.
- Green: Safety, harmony, freshness, nature, health and wealth.
- Orange: Enthusiasm, cheerfulness, creativity, playfulness, vibrant and heat.
- Pink: Nurture, sweet, soft, romance, caring and security.
- Purple: Power, wealth, nobility, intelligence, magic, sensuality and spirituality.
- Red: Boldness, excitement, urgency, desire, intensity, danger and love.
- Silver: Scientific, cold, prestige, sleekness, modernity and high-tech.
- White: Cleanliness, purity, simplicity, peace and innocence.

- Yellow: Attention-grabbing, happiness, warmth, energy, joy and optimism.

People will judge your business by your website and your branding. Take some time to think through what image and personality you want to reflect to the world.

Chapter Summary

Your digital branding is more than just how your website looks. It is the sum of the online perceptions, memories and experiences that people have of your products or company.

The six major elements of digital branding include: targeting, logo, domain name, personality, visibility and consistency.

A good logo is simple, distinctive, represents the company and has the illusion of action.

Your domain should be memorable, recognizable and easy to type out.

Color is a powerful visual communicator that creates an emotional and memorable response.

Website Planning Steps

- ☐ Settle on your domain name.
- ☐ Decide if you will keep or update your logo. Then get a high resolution version for use in your website design.
- ☐ Decide what colors to use in branding.

4 Closing the Deal

Most business websites today do little to generate leads or sales. The reason is because they are not designed to interact with their visitors. Most are just a brochure with basic information about the business. The hope is somebody will be interested enough to pick up the phone and call.

These are what I call the average business websites.

What separates an average website from top producing business websites? It is focusing and targeting the needs of your buyer.

Your website's appearance, messaging and your offer need to target their needs. You need to understand the psychology and motivation of these buyers. People come to your website to solve a specific problem.

To Dominate Ask These 4 Questions

1. What- What is the focus of your site? What products or services do you offer? Your website, like your business needs to have a clear purpose. What problems do you solve for your buyers? How is it unique and better than your competition? What benefits will your buyer experience by buying from you? Your home page should address and answer those questions.

2. Who- Who are your best buyers? What do you know about them? How old are they? How well educated? Income level? Live or work in a particular area? From a particular industry? Create a realistic profile of your best buyer. Use this persona to visualize what their triggers are.
3. Why- Why would they come? What are their motivations? What personal desires are they trying to satisfy? What are their pain points? Are you closely matching their needs with what you have to offer?
4. Action- What makes them buy? What is the trigger that will cause them to buy? By showing that you clearly understand their pain, people become much more open to buying. You want to present a website that clearly solves their issue. Make it clear and easy this path to action.

Drive your visitors toward a desired action. Online viewers can only focus on one thing at a time. If you present many options, then they won't react to any of them.

Getting people who come to your site to take specific actions is called conversion optimization.

"Conversion" means to persuade individuals you have attracted to your website to voluntarily undertake one or more action steps. Depending upon the goals you have established for your website, this may mean you want them to sign up for a newsletter, make a purchase, fill out a form or perhaps simply contact you.

Four Elements of Conversion Optimization

1. The purpose of the website- This is your business objective for creation of the site. It may be to attract leads, make a sale, build your email list, reach out to a given niche of potential customers, etc.
2. Ideal buyer profile- This is a profile and description of those individuals you want to attract to your website. You need to understand who they are, their motivations, what triggers them and how they typically make buying decisions.
3. Conversion- Your website must present you, your message and your brand in a compelling and positive manner. Ideally, it expresses your value proposition clearly and persuasively, solves a critical problem and effectually guides the potential buyer to take the action steps you desire.
4. Traffic- Your website must attract a continual stream of desirable visitors who are good conversion candidates. The winning tactic is to reach out to those individuals who are already searching for what you offer, but to do it more effectively than your competition.

Incorporating just the right blend of logic, emotion, science, psychology and art into a website is the formula to attract prospects who are interested in what you offer, have a current need, can afford to buy now, and will buy again in the future.

B2B vs B2C

Buying behavior differs greatly between businesses (B2B) and consumers (B2C).

Business-to-Consumer Buyers: The B2C buyer makes a more impulsive decision based on their current need. This includes product, value, cost, and status. Buying is based on a desire with a very short decision making time. Most consumers will buy regularly from stores and locations that they like. B2C marketing needs to build trust and loyalty with their customers.

Business-to-Business Buyers: Perhaps the biggest difference with the B2B buyer is the sales cycle. Usually many people are involved with the decision to purchase something. The business buyer is typically much more knowledgeable about the product than a consumer and will often spend more time doing analysis before making their decision. A company marketing to businesses needs to focus on relationship building and communication using marketing activities that generate leads that can be nurtured during the sales cycle.

If your website markets to B2B buyers, then your primary action needs to be to get their email address with a free report, an eBook or even in a quote request. You need to focus on ways to nurture the relationship and work toward closing the deal.

Often, this is done by email using what is called drip marketing. Drip marketing is ideal for selling big ticket items where there is a long sales cycle.

Figure 4.1 Drip Marketing

> ***Example of drip marketing:*** *Let's say your company sales $200,000 machine tools to industrial businesses. The buying cycle is typically 6 months. You may place a free report on your website made to appeal to industrial buyers such as: "The 7 Critical Mistakes Industrial Buyers Make in Purchasing Industrial Machine Tools."*
>
> *When they sign up to receive the free report, you deliver the download link via email. You would then follow up with weekly emails for 6-9 months educating them further on purchasing tips for machine tools. Each email would encourage them to contact your company for a consultation and a quote.*

Prospects will generally sign-up for some sort of free offer on your website. The free report or digital download is automatically delivered. Follow-up messages are sent out using sequential auto responders. The email messages are pre-written in a planned sequence and sent out at planned intervals such as once a week or every 3 days.

You are trying to encourage prospects to interact and engage with you. You are educating and providing information that your best buyer would find helpful. You are providing relevant content that will grab the attention of these future customers.

The idea is to deliver information that a prospects would consider of value. This could take the form of an e-course or a series of emails designed to help your prospect solve some problem or issue. To be successful, drip marketing keeps the basic messaging the same, but each communication is fresh and interesting to your recipient.

The goal is to build brand awareness. It fixes your brand and company name in your potential customer's mind.

If your website focusses on B2C buyers, then go directly for the sale. Use drip marketing to sell related products. Capture email addresses so you can continually remarket to them with newsletters and announcements of sales to get them to become repeat buyers.

The Selling Sequence

Every business has a sales process that best guides your prospects into becoming buyers. Your website is no different. You need to design your selling sequence that will grab their attention, build their interest and then get them to take action.

How you present information to visitors to convert them from a prospect to a customer is your sales process. Your selling sequence should follow AIDA. This is Attention, Interest, Desire and then Action. This has been in use as a sales training tool for over a hundred years. For good reason, it works.

The typical selling sequence starts by making the prospect aware of your product. You then spend time generating interest in what you are selling. You then stimulate the desire to possess the product. Finally you encourage the prospect to buy.

A visitor begins by arriving to your website because they are searching for a solution to their need. If you start by demonstrating what your product can do, then the customer may not want that capability you are offering. If you first create interest and then desire for your product, then they feel they have to have what you are selling.

You have to develop the need. You do this by first asking questions in a way where your product or service is the natural answer to the question. Do this with the right questions and then you develop a genuine need for your product.

If you have several pricing levels, which do you present first? You would present your highest priced, premium priced products of course.

The airlines are pros at this. Think of how you enter the plane on the way to Economy. First you get on the plane and walk through First Class. You see the wide comfortable seats, all the amenities, even drinks being served before takeoff. Next you march past business class; then you arrive in Economy.

Pricing for First Class gives sticker shock, and most of us say no to the high prices. Then every time we enter the plane, we are guided through the sequence of Attention, then Interest and then Desire. This helps trigger Action when we finally get fed up with Economy and "bang", they have a sell.

You may need to create multiple buyer personas. You can then design separate optimal selling sequences and then guide each persona through their buying process.

To develop your selling sequence you need to thoroughly understand your buyer, what problem they are trying to solve and what their buying criteria are. You will need to adapt this general 10 step sales process to your website.

1. Identify your buyer(s). You may need to develop multiple personas if you have several different customers that you market to.
2. How are you going to get interested prospects to your website?
3. What specific problem is each buyer trying to find a solution for?
4. How does your product or service solve this problem? How is it unique and better than your competition? What benefits will your buyer experience by buying from you?

5. What action do you want the visitor to take that would constitute success for you? How will you measure this?
6. How will you grab their attention and pique a potential customer's interest?
7. What concerns will a buyer have that might cause them to put off a purchase? What can you do to build trust and reduce risk for a prospect?
8. What is the best way to present what you sell to the prospect? This should be as a solution to their problem and in a way that benefits them the most.
9. What is the trigger that will cause a prospect to buy? How do you overcome objections? How will you close the sale?
10. How will you service and follow up with these customers so you can turn them into repeat buyers?

As you plan your website, develop a selling sequence for each type of buyer. Think about these steps as potentially separate web pages that you want to guide your visitor through.

B2B Sales

B2B (business-to-business) sales generally has a long selling cycle and you need to design in some sort of interaction strategy. This is could be a free report that allows you to collect email addresses and then follow up with sequential auto responders. Another alternative is adding a request a quote form to your website.

Call to Actions

Your call-to-action needs to answer three questions.

1. **What?** What should they do? What action do you want them to take? Buy? Request a quote? Make an appointment? Sign-up?
2. **Why?** Why should they do it? How will it benefit them?
3. **How?** How do they take action? What is the next step?

5 attributes of a great call to action

1. Compelling- Make sure it satisfies a real need your visitor has. Use action oriented phrases such a "Buy Now" or "Join Today."
2. Visible- Location is very important. Make it clearly visible and above the fold. Use colors that make it stand out. On your home page, the upper right quadrant is prime territory for your call to action. It is more easily seen there.
3. Clarity- Keep it simple. Use short bulleted phrases. Don't clutter it up with too much text. Use simple graphics. Use ample white space.
4. Urgency- Create a sense of urgency to encourage immediate action. Limit the time or the quantity. Have

an expiration date or label it as a limited time offer. You could make the offer available for the first 30 buyers.
5. Incentive- Offer a premium or reward for taking immediate action. This could be "Act now and receive..." Use an incentive that will appeal to your best buyer. This will help attract your targeted customer.

As you plan your website you will want to create a list of all possible actions that you want visitors to do. This could be to sign up for a free report, request a quote or even call for more information. You will want to prioritize this list from the most important to the least important.

You will make your highest priority action the most visible and the most compelling.

Do People Trust your Website?

The single most important factor is first impression. Does your website look professional, organized and credible? People do judge a book by its cover. If your website looks like it was put together by an amateur, then that will be their perception of your business.

A study by researchers in Canada[7] showed that people form lasting judgments about the usability and credibility of a website in as little as 1/20th of a second. The reaction is a physiological and emotional response based on color, images, page load speed and organization. This first impression was not based on informational content.

A well-organized website is inviting and encourages people to come in and look around. Avoid strong and oppressive colors. Design with a minimum number of different fonts.

It is no difference with the brick and mortar stores that you shop in. Would you prefer to shop at a small store with a few items for sale, where the merchandise is not well organized, the shopping area not well lit, things are hard to find and where the checkout stand is a long complicated process?

Or would you rather shop at a store with good selection, well organized into departments, well lit with wide aisles and a quick and easy checkout?

Make your website inviting to your visitor.

Avoid a long list of categories that extend down the left sidebar. The human mind will not easily track more than a dozen categories. If you have 20-30 categories, reorganize them into higher level categories. You want to reduce the number of options a visitor has to choose from. Seven is optimal, but never have more than twelve categories.

Use videos whenever possible. Visitors like to view video content. Add how-to videos to allow people to visualize the product in use or even how to assemble it.

Your website needs to develop that instant trust that comes from that visual first impression. Then follow up with more signs they should trust you. Here are more ideas.

Appearance: The design of the website must be professional, uncluttered and have a neat visual appearance. Content and navigation must be organized and clear. Use high quality images to communicate your message.

Transactional Assurances: Show buyers there is no risk in doing business with your company. Provide assurances with privacy policies, guarantees, forms of payments accepted, return policies and trust logos. Provide point of action assurances with brief statements or links to your policies on privacy, guarantees and returns. Include your phone number and address on every page.

Authority Symbols: Your website must contain symbols of authority and credibility. People will immediately trust someone with a badge and a gun or a doctor in a white smock. With visual assurances people will make quick decisions with very limited information. For medical sites use photos of doctors in white coats and stethoscopes. Add trust logos such as BBBonline or industry associations.

Social Proof: Provide third party recommendations with video and written testimonials. Integrate social reviews and comments using product reviews, ratings, consumer feedback, wish-lists, favorites, blogs, forums or chat rooms.

Closing the deal on your website uses what is called Conversion Rate Optimization. This is a blend of art and science. Your website must be professional and credible; it must be trustworthy, solve their problem and have a clear path to action.

Education Based Marketing

Traditional websites tend to be promotional causing visitors to put up their defenses against being sold to. It is like walking onto a car sales lot and immediately being approached by a commission only sales person. You know their mission is to get the sale. You also know there will be a barrage of sales tactics all designed to extract the highest price from you.

A better approach is to use education based marketing. Educate your visitors using fact filled content to help them make a better informed buying decision. Education based marketing is not a sales pitch. Use market data to engage prospects and show that your company is the logical one to do business with.

The idea is to educate buyers about their future purchase using market research data and market trends. You will educate them so they can make a well informed purchase decision and avoid making a decision they will regret. After all the lowest priced product is frequently not the lowest cost when everything is taken into account.

The Educational Process

Start with identifying what makes your company, product or service different than your competition. This is often your unique selling proposition (USP) that differentiates you from your competition.

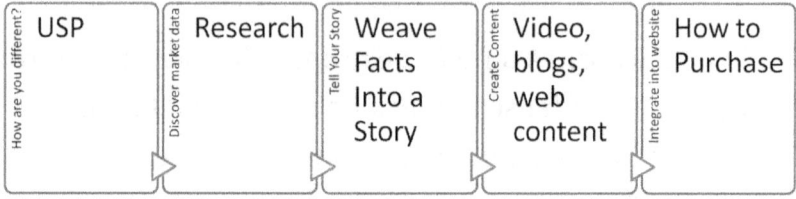

Figure 4.2 Educational Marketing Process

You will do market research to use statistics and consumer experiences to show the pitfalls and problem with buying the other products or services. You then spend time educating your website visitor about potential problems and how you have a unique solution.

You build this information into your website content. This approach builds trust and positions you as the authority.

Traditional advertising generates a very low level of trust. Instead companies are turning to education based marketing where they teach, educate and even entertain. They are doing this by creating content that their best buyers will want to read.

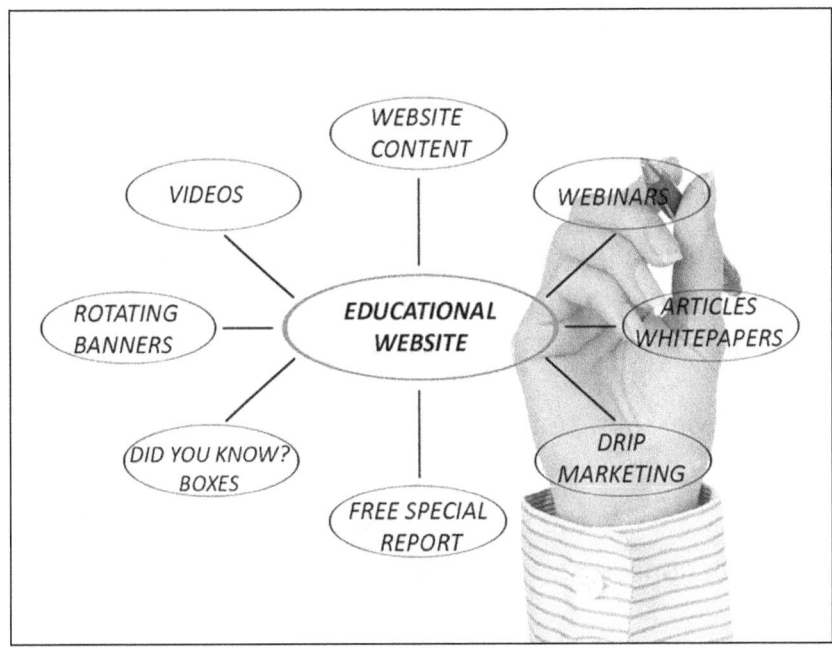

Figure 4.3 Integrating Educational Elements

Marketers must rise to this challenge and they must produce content designed to engage and inspire. Here are 10 ways to use educational marketing in your website.

1. Messaging- Write your market statistics into your page content. Educate web visitors on hidden trends and problems in making purchases in your market. Show how you are part of the solution. Weave market data into your marketing message.

2. Rotating Banners- On your home page, include graphical banner images. Include attention getting statistics to engage your visitor.

3. Videos- Create 2-4 minute videos that inform and educate. When presented by your CEO it puts a friendly face on the company.

4. Free Report- Create a free report that can be used as a sign-up incentive for building your email list. Make the title of your report compelling so that buyers of your products / services are intrigued.

5. Drip Marketing Campaign- This is an email campaign where pre-written emails are delivered at regular intervals. Use the market facts and statistics to write educational emails to people that sign-up to your email list.

6. Articles- Write and publish articles that will position you as a leader in your market. Always include a link back to your website in your byline at the end of the article.

7. Blogging- Add a blog to your website and use the market data content as the basis for many posts.

8. Social Media- Spice up your Facebook page and create compelling tweets using educational content.

9. Did You Know- Add "Did you know?" boxes on each page of your website. Include interesting facts and statistics about your niche. This is really effective in engaging visitors in your website.

10. Webinars- Put on live webinars and allow sign-ups on your website. As an alternative, have a recorded version of your webinar that visitors can sign-up for and then watch at their convenience.

Chapter Summary

Your website needs selling sequence that will grab their attention, build their interest and then get them to take action. You may have multiple selling sequences for multiple buyer personas.

Call to actions should be compelling, visible, clear, have a sense of urgency and can have an incentive if they signup.

Your website needs to develop that instant trust that comes from that visual first impression. Use your phone number and address on every page, add trust logos and include product reviews and customer feedback.

Use education based marketing to better connect with your website visitors. Use market data to engage prospects and show that your company is the logical one to do business with.

Website Planning Steps

- ☐ Map out selling sequences for each buyer type.
- ☐ Create a prioritized list of actions for visitors.
- ☐ List out ways you will reassure visitors and build trust
- ☐ Create an inventory of videos you plan on using.
- ☐ Integrate educational marketing?

5 Size-up Your Competition

It is in looking at your competition's websites that your vision will become clear on how you will want your website to look and what calls to action you will want. This is one of the most important steps in planning your new website.

You can get the best ideas of what to include in your website by studying your competition. You want your website to be better than your competitors. You can get ideas for designs, layouts, calls to actions, offers, functionality and why they are attracting traffic.

Remember your customers will be searching through a great many websites and comparing your website to your competition. The objective is to pick and choose the best ideas and improve on them so that your business will be the obvious choice to buy from.

In this chapter we will discuss how to do your own completive analysis and what you should be looking for. We will share our approach when we use with our clients. Our approach is look through many websites and select the pieces and parts of websites where others are doing things in the very best way and ignore the things they are doing poorly.

How to select competitive websites

Start by creating a list of companies that you consider your direct competition. Limit this to only 3-5 companies. Locate their websites and add these to your list.

In addition, you want to choose others by doing searches on Google.

Go to the keyword research that you did from chapter 2. You will want to pick the 5 best phrases that describe the services or products that you provide. These will become the "power phrases" that you will want to use in uncovering your competition.

This will be the same way your customers will be searching for you. You want to be seeing what they see.

To find competitors do a Google search using your "power keywords". Limit yourself to websites you find on the first two pages of Google.

As you do this search and you may notice the websites coming up are not a competitor to what you offer, if this is the case, then you may want to substitute a different keyword phrase that brings up better results. Make a note of this substitution so you can use this as you create your SEO page plan in chapter 6.

In the first pass you will be quickly going through these websites and sorting the good ones that you like from the "ugly" ones that you don't like.

Be prepared for a lot of "ugly" websites. Usually I reject at least 90% of the websites I look at in this first sort. If you are real picky, then you may reject 98% of the websites.

The goal in this first pass is to create a pool of good websites. You will look at these and select the best websites to become your reference websites. These will help guide the web designer in building your new website.

What to Look for in These Competitor Websites

The first pass as I said is to sort the good from the ugly. You are not trying to find the perfect website, only good ones. As you look closely at the good ones later, you will find pieces or elements that you really like that you want to include into your website.

This first sort is a quick visual sort and I look for three things to label a website as "good".

1. First Impression
2. Good layout
3. Clear call-to-actions

First impression- What is your initial reaction in the first 1-2 seconds? Does the page load quickly? This will be an emotional "I like it" or "I hate it". If you hate it, go onto the next website, if you like it try and figure out why.

The design should look professional but not overpowering. Do they see the most important things first?

Good Layout- This includes the page structure or where the elements are placed. Is it well organized? Is the navigation understandable? How clearly is the message presented? Can you find the information you need without scrolling down the page?

Clear call-to-action- Are there clear actions for visitors to take? This could be to request an appointment, signup for a newsletter or to call. Are the calls to actions placed so you can see them on the home page without scrolling down? Best practices are to place the call to actions in the upper right quadrant of the home page. See the example on the next page.

If you like a particular website for all three of these categories, then you will want to save it for further analysis.

An easy way to save these is to take a screenshot and paste them onto a Word document or into PowerPoint.

Looking for an easy to use way to grab screenshots? I use free software called Jing.
http://www.techsmith.com/jing.html This makes it very easy to save examples of sites you like for future

review. Be sure to type in the web address of each screen shot so you can find the website in the future.

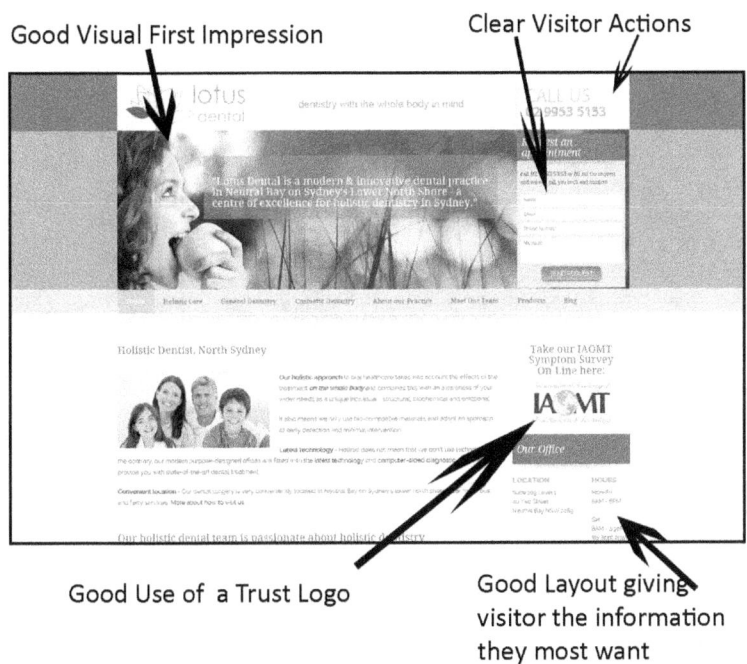

Figure 5.1 http://www.lotusdental.com.au

Further Analysis

If you end up saving 10-15 "good" websites that you like the layout on, then you will have enough of a pool to select your top 3-5 reference websites.

The easiest way to make your selections is to rate each website on how well you like them for each of the three categories. I will rate them 1-10 with ten being best. See the example rating sheet.

Website URL	First Impression	Good Layout	Clear CTA	Total Score
lotusdental.com.au	10	9	10	29
lighthousedental.net	6	7	7	20
mitchmarderdds.com	7	5	8	20

You will also want to take notes on your favorite 3-5 websites and what you like about them. This will help the designer when they create your design.

Below are typical comments when referring to a specific website. These are actual client comments taken from some of our past projects that we included to help the designers.

1. I like the colors, images and visual design great but it is a poor layout

2. I like the layout, simplicity and the overall design
3. I like how they did the buttons on right side
4. Visually clean with a nice appearance. Looks professional
5. I hate the colors; I like the location of the call to action and layout
6. Visually poor and lacks organization. I do like how four problems are presented on the home page
7. I like the look of the website, clean, white look… but it is not designed well for conversion
8. Good organization, structure and layout. Professional graphic design
9. I like how video was included in rotating banner
10. I loved the slanted pictures, but I don't like the black in the header

Select one website that you liked the layout of. This can become the basis of planning your layout. Remember the layout is how the elements are arranged not the visual design i.e. colors. By elements we mean things such as navigation, top banner image, call to actions, how the text is organized into boxes, where videos are placed, etc.

If you narrow it down to two websites and know exactly how you'd combine them for your layout; create a rough sketch.

Functions and Features

As you look at competitor websites, identify features that you like and want to include on your website. Some common ones include-

1. Rotating top banner (commonly called a slider).
2. Ability to add videos into top slider
3. Events calendar
4. Photo gallery
5. Email capture forms with autoresponder.
6. Email capture forms integrated to email system such as Mailchimp, Aweber or Constant Contact. Use on newsletter subscriptions, etc.
7. CAPTCHA added to forms. A CAPTCHA helps prevent spam submitted by robots. It is a series of numbers or letters filled in before submitting a web form.
8. Knowledgebase instead of a traditional FAQ page
9. eCommerce store
10. Surveys or polls

11. Google Maps and driving directions

12. Feedback forms to gather information

Identify the functions and features that you want to include in your website.

The review you just completed compared the look and feel, call to actions and the features to include in your website.

Traffic Review

How good of job is your competition doing at attracting traffic to their website? How are they doing it? Compare their results to yours. The traffic review is designed to show this.

Create a list of your competitor websites that you want to check. Usually you want to compare your website against 3-5 competitor websites.

Adding the SEOQuake toolbar to your browser makes this analysis much quicker to do. https://www.seoquake.com/

Prepare a spreadsheet so you tabulate your results. See the example below.

Measurement	Your website	Competitor 1	Competitor 2
Alexa Ranking			
Pages Indexed (Google)			

Pageload speed (mobile)			
Pageload speed (Desktop)			
External Backlinks			
Referring Domains			
Current keywords			

Alexa Ranking- This is an indication of the traffic volume going to each website. A lower number means a higher volume of traffic. Use the SEOQuake toolbar.

Pages Indexed (Google) - How big is the website? How many pages are indexed by Google? Larger websites tend to attract more traffic, due to higher amounts of keyword rich content. Use the SEOQuake tool bar to get this information. If your website has fewer pages; this may indicate a need for a content growth strategy.

Page Load Speed- This tool analyzes how fast a web page loads on mobile and desktops and gives recommendations to fix. A higher number indicates a faster load time. Load speed is part of Google search algorithm.
http://developers.google.com/speed/pagespeed/insights/

External Backlinks- This is a measure of link popularity and is the number of links from other websites that link back to a website. Higher is better. Use https://www.majesticseo.com to measure this using the Fresh index option.

Referring Domains- This shows how many unique domains are linking back to a given website. Higher is better. Use https://www.majesticseo.com to measure this using the Fresh index option.

Current keywords- Which keyword phrases is the website currently ranked for? Are they using paid search to bring in traffic? This can give you ideas for keywords that you will want to target. Use http://www.spyfu.com.

By entering this information into a spreadsheet, you will quickly see how your website measures up to the competition and who your primary competition is.

Use the traffic review to decide what you need to do to be a leader in your market. If you need a larger website, perhaps add a blog. If you need more external links, then you will need a way to attract these links (See chapter 10).

Chapter Summary

You can get the best ideas of what to include in your website by studying your competition. You can get ideas for designs, layouts, calls-to-actions, offers, functionality and why they are attracting traffic.

The first review is to identify reference websites that will help the designer get a vision of what you want in a website design. You may scan through a hundred websites to select the best 3-5 based on first impression, good layout and clear call-to-action.

The second type of review is the traffic review to uncover how your competition is attracting website traffic. Use this to plan your own traffic strategies.

––––––––––––––

Website Planning Steps

- ☐ List 3-5 reference websites. Include comments of what you like and what you don't like.
- ☐ List of functions and features to include
- ☐ Do a competitive traffic review and compare your website to your competition.

6 Create Your Website Plan

You will want to gather all of your plans for your new website into a document that is called the design brief. Building this design brief allows you to consider and plan all the key elements for your website.

This also serves as a set of instructions for your web developer making sure they will be able to produce the website that your business needs.

The Design Brief

The format can differ, but the key elements remain the same. This is the design brief format that we use in planning websites for our clients.

Prepare a formal written document that includes-

1. **Domain and Website Logins.** This will give the developers the access to the current site and to make the new website live.

    a. Website URL

    b. Domain Registrar and domain login

    c. Current website FTP and admin panel login

    d. Google Analytics and Webmaster Tools logins

2. **Description and Objectives**- These items form a summary of the project. Each item should only be about one paragraph in length.

    a. Business Description- What services / products does the business provide, positioning, major marketing initiatives and 2 year goals.

    b. Project Description- Describe any special functionality, custom programming or data importing that must be done as part of the project. Any modules that should be deployed? Integration with Facebook?

    c. Website Objectives- What business results do you expect from the website? Examples would be lead generation, online sales, build image and credibility. List in priority order if more than one.

    d. Mobile- How important is mobile? What are mobile visitor priorities?

3. **Targeted Audience**. If you have more than one buyer profile, list your best buyer first. Should be one paragraph per buyer and include buying triggers.

4. **Design Information**

    a. Design objectives- Any design boundaries or specific look wanted?

    b. Colors- List any colors that are part of company branding. Are there colors that you definitely want or colors that must be avoided? If you have a specific color, specify the HTML color number or take a screen shot of the color on a website.

    c. Logo- Provide the designer a high resolution copy of the logo. Will a tagline or slogan be used?

    d. Provide a list of 3-5 reference websites. Describe what specifically you like about each. This gives the designer insight into what you like.

    e. Interior page designs- How many separate interior page design layouts do you want? Typical is one.

    f. Landing page- Will landing pages be needed for PPC campaigns?

    If you are going to advertise using Google AdWords or any other type of PPC advertising; always send your traffic to a well-designed landing page. This will increase your conversion rate and decrease your cost per lead or sale.

Types of Pages

Home Page
This is the main entrance page into the website. It's main job is to orient and direct the visitor deeper into the website.

Interior Page
These are the sub pages within the website. They carry the main content in the site.

Landing Pages
These are simplified pages with little to no navigation. Used in PPC campaigns to get higher conversion rates.

Figure 6.1 Types of Web Pages

5. **Conversion plans**- These are your plans to reassure and get visitors to take action.

    a. Trust elements- Describe strategies to build trust with the visitor. This would include trust logos.

Privacy and returns policies, customer reviews, etc

b. Social Media link locations- Which social media icons to include? The most common ones are Google+, Twitter, Facebook, YouTube, Pinterest, LinkedIn

c. Call-to-actions- Provide a prioritized list from the most important to the least important

d. Provide a list of videos that will be used along with a link to where they are hosted. i.e. YouTube or Vimeo

e. Is there a free report or eBook that will be offered as part of your email list building?

f. Email list- Will emails collected need to be added to an existing list? If so, where is this list maintained? Examples- Aweber, Constant Contact, MailChimp

g. eCommerce? Will there be online product or service sales? How will payments be taken? Which payment gateway, merchant account provider are you using?

6. **Content writing**- Who will be writing the content for the website? You can write it yourself or hire a professional writer. Don't expect a web developer to write for you.

Someone who is a marketer should do the writing. The developer will need the content before they create the design to incorporate it into the design layout.

   a. Web pages

   b. Landing pages

   c. Auto responder emails.

   d. Email drip campaign emails.

7. Sitemap and SEO page plan

8. Wireframe

More information about how to individual items in the design brief can be found elsewhere in this book.

How to Create Your Sitemap and SEO Plan

A sitemap is a listing of the pages and subpages to be included in your website. It shows how they relate to each other.

The flow of your website should follow your natural selling process. When you design your website structure, begin by thinking like a customer.

This is actually "story-boarding" your sales presentation. Having a picture of your whole web site will make it easier to create a menu system that is useful to your visitors.

Let's say you have a restaurant and you want a 12 page website. You would start by listing out the topics that would answer the questions your visitors would have.

For a restaurant a visitor may want to know-

What makes the restaurant special and different than others in the area?

- What's their menu and pricing?
- Can I make a reservation?
- Will the food work with my diet?
- Where are they located and what are their hours?
- Can I get a job there?
- Do they sell gift cards?

This is a site map that would answer these questions.

1		Home page
1		Our Menus
	2	Lunch
	2	Dinner
	2	Wine List
	2	Nutritional information
1		Delivery
1		Catering and Banquets
1		About Us
	2	Careers
1		Directions and hours
1		Purchase a Gift Card

1. Start by listing out the pages to include. Avoid using obscure names for your pages; it will only confuse your visitors. Your Home Page should explain what you provide and why they should choose you. The About Us page should talk about your history, mission, vision and values.

2. Primary pages to be included in the main navigation are listed with a "1". Subpages may be a "2" or "3".

3. Group pages that cover the same general subject. Then order them according to how people will look for them. For example, people will first look for the menu and then ask about the nutritional values.

4. The sequence of topics should match your best sales process. In the site map above, the visitor would look first at the Home Page. Then they would want to see the menu and learn about the restaurant (About Us). Finally they would want to see where they are located and their hours.

Once you have a listing of pages, use the keywords from your research and match the most relevant phrases with each page. Right now, focus on one primary phrase per page. This will serve as a guide for your content writing.

Restaurants are searched for by location so include the city in the keywords. See example below.

Level		Page Name	Primary keyword
1		Home page	italian restaurant denver
1		Our Menus	italian restaurant menu
	2	Lunch	italian lunch menu denver
	2	Dinner	italian dinner menu denver
	2	Wine List	wine list denver
	2	Nutritional information	nutritional information
1		Delivery	local restaurants that deliver
1		Catering and Banquets	italian catering denver
1		About Us	italian food denver
	2	Careers	restaurant jobs denver
1		Directions and hours	local italian restaurant
1		Purchase a Gift Card	restaurant gift cards

SEO Plan

To create the full SEO plan, you will need to expand the sitemap example above. This will give the instructions the web developer needs to apply the important META tags to each web page.

1. Level (already on sitemap)
2. Page name to display on the menu (already on sitemap)
3. Primary keyword phrase (already on sitemap)
4. Secondary keyword
5. Title Tag
6. META Description
7. H1 Tag (main page headlines)

Details for how to create Title tags, META Description and H1 tags are discussed in Chapter 10 under the organic SEO section.

Multiple Selling Sequences

What happens when you have customers with very different needs? Then you would want to establish multiple selling paths.

Let's suppose you are a flooring retailer that sells to residential consumers, residential building contractors and commercial buyers. You would have three different types of customers, each with different needs and buying criteria. Don't try and sell to all three groups on the same web page.

Develop three different sales paths clearly on the home page. Each sales path addresses the needs, problems and concerns for a specific buying group.

- The residential consumer is after quality, service and quick installation

- The building contractor looks for budget pricing and extreme flexibility for installation scheduling

- The commercial buyer is looking for commercial quality and service contracts

By establishing a separate sales page for each, you can address the specific needs for that customer.

How to create a wireframe

A website wireframe is a schematic view of your web page layout. This is kind of a "first draft" used in planning and organizing a web page. It is a skeletal rendering of how the web page elements fit together onto the page.

Wireframing is generally done with grayscale block diagrams that illustrate the overall navigation and blocks of elements such as images, content and functionality. The call-to-actions are strategically located. These are organizational plans and not a completed design. They are done before any artwork is generated.

The term "wireframe" comes from the world of computer graphics and 3D animation. Here wireframes are used for prototyping and because they are quick to generate and they use a minimum of computer processing.

Wireframes can be created with many different computer programs. It does not require special software. I typically use Photoshop, but I have seen wireframes created in many different graphics programs. I have seen standard office programs such as Excel or Word. What are important are the positions of the key elements.

Using a planning wireframe will often generate new requirements and questions that hadn't been thought of before. It forces you to think through your website's functionality at the page level. Creating a sitemap and wireframe are essential steps before doing a website design.

1. Determine the basic layout such as how many columns the page will have. Should the navigation be along the top (horizontal) or on the side (vertical)?

2. Decide on the call to action for the page. Place it where it can be easily seen, preferably above the fold so it can be seen immediately by an arriving visitor without scrolling down.

3. Organize and place the page elements such as the header, footer, navigation, content objects, and branding elements. Group and prioritize the elements according to how you want them seen.

4. Label the navigation links, headings and content objects.

5. Use placeholders for text and images. Use dummy text such as lorem ipsum to show text areas.

The wireframe gives your web designer a visual guide to layout. This ensures the call to action and priority elements are placed on the page for maximum effectiveness.

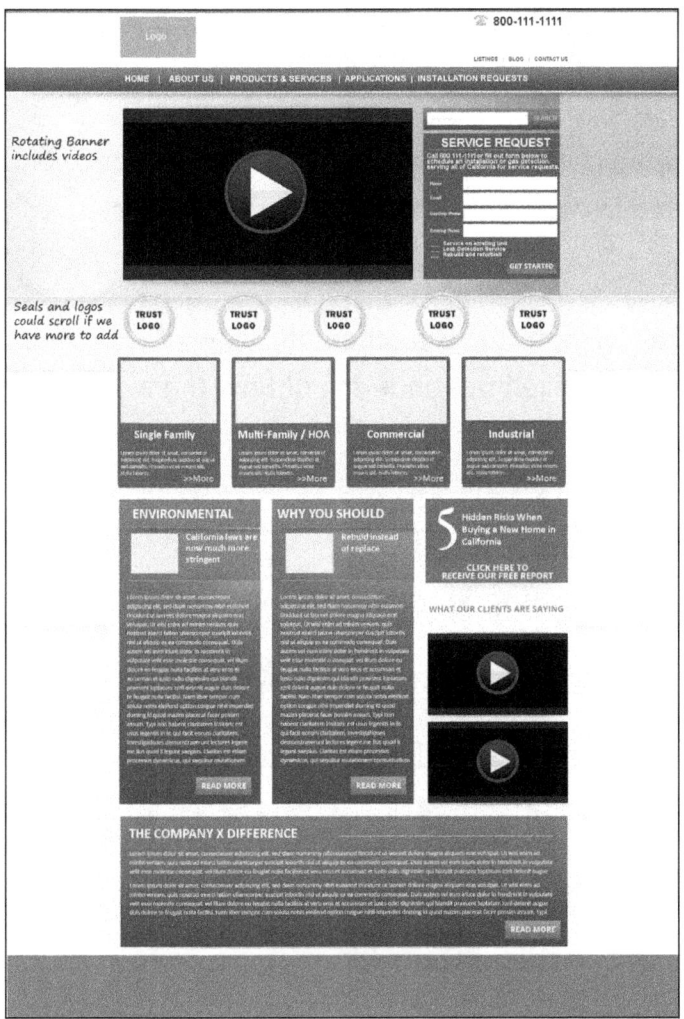

Figure 6.2 Example of a Wireframe

Chapter Summary

You will want to gather all of your plans for your new website into a document that is called the design brief.

Building this design brief allows you to consider and plan all the key elements for your website.

A sitemap is a listing of the pages and subpages to be included in your website. It shows how they relate to each other.

A website wireframe is a schematic view of your web page layout. It is a skeletal rendering of how the web page elements fit together onto the page.

Website Planning Steps

- ☐ Create the sitemap for your website.
- ☐ Create the SEO Plan for your website
- ☐ Create the wireframe for your home page
- ☐ Prepare the design brief completing as much information as possible.

7 Crafting Your Message

Marketing with your website is less about technology and more about marketing. A website that produces sales is much more than a great looking design.

It speaks to the needs of your best buyer, acknowledges their problem and demonstrates that you are absolutely the best solution for them.

You are educating and providing information that customers would find helpful. You are providing relevant content that will grab the attention of these future customers. You tell your story using words, pictures and videos.

Writing for the web is different than writing for print. Write content for your website that is brief and to the point with shorter paragraphs, shorter sentences and fewer words, than a printed version.

People will read something more completely when it is written on paper and only skim information that is presented on the screen. They tend to ignore details, reading short paragraphs, headlines or bulleted lists.

> **Example**: The Above paragraph rewritten for the web.
>
> People only skim info on the screen
>
> - They ignore details
> - Only read short paragraphs
> - Read headlines
> - Read bulleted lists

Why? They are able to read a paper document 25% faster. It is physically harder to read from the screen. It is harder on the eyes. There are a lot of reasons for this such as sharpness of font, font size, contrast, position of the screen.

In print you can control the reader from introduction to conclusion. With web content the visitor is in control and they choose their own path of what to read next. They follow navigation and links according to what interests them.

On the screen, few people read everything on a page. Most will scan a page looking for the information they are after. They skip whole blocks of text, particularly longer paragraphs.

The same way a graphic designer will call attention to elements with color, a web copywriter highlights with format and structure. This means headlines, using **bold**, bulleted lists, etc. Information in larger paragraphs is more hidden.

12 content writing tips

1. Solutions- People are looking for solutions and answers rather than to learn about your company. Focus on the benefits and answer your visitor's questions "So, what's in it for me?" "What am I doing here," "How do I do it," and "Where can I go next?"

2. Targeted- Your message should connect with your targeted buyer. Don't try and reach everyone who could possibly need your service. Go after your best buyer. Address the specific needs of that customer and how you will solve a problem of directly benefit them. Ask yourself, "How will what I offer make my customer's life better?"

3. It's about them- Spend less time writing about your company and answer how you will solve their problem. Remember, your primary duty is to give them what they need.

4. Benefits- Write about the benefits. Benefits are what sell. Benefits are what features mean. Features are what products do.

5. Get their attention- When they first arrive, they need to immediately see your sales pitch, your offering and even your order button. Don't make them scroll down or switch pages.

6. Back up what you say- Web visitors don't believe hype. If you want to be believable, you have to back it up. Reference your sources.

7. 3 Second Rule- Internet users are active, not passive. If they don't immediately see what they are looking for, they are gone within 3 seconds. First impressions are critical.

8. Be brief- Use shorter sentences, words and paragraphs. Use one idea per paragraph and use about half the words than you would use in writing for print.

9. Active Voice- Write concisely, plainly and openly. Write using action oriented words to get your message across as quickly as possible. Speak to your reader's emotions and engage them with your words. Don't be elusive or try to reach everyone. Instead of saying, "Our service will help you be more effective in your marketing efforts." Try saying, "Dominate and close 30% more sales with our service."

Make your content easy and quick to digest. Write your content so it can be understood by a third grade

reading level. You are writing to be understood, not to impress.

10. Start strong and finish strong- Grab their attention when they arrive, and astound them with your finish. Put your best material at the beginning and the end.

11. Easy to scan- Your reader wants to scan down your web page and get the gist of it before reading. The main points should stand out in sub-headlines, lists, images, colors, italics and indented text.

12. Action- Your visitor arrives ready to take action. Tell them what to do. Make your call to action clearly visible. If someone arrives and then leaves without taking some action, what have you accomplished?

Good content writing entertains, educates and convinces your audience. By skillfully weaving in keywords, content writing also gets the attention of the search engines.

Writing for SEO

You want your website to be found when people do a Google search. You do this by incorporating keywords into each page of your website. You will use the sitemap – SEO plan that you prepared in the last chapter.

SEO is about optimizing a website for people that use search engines. It is this human side of search engine optimization. Use keywords as a central theme in your messaging, your page headlines and your hyperlinks. It is about establishing relevance to what your visitors are searching for.

Targeted keyword phrases are weaved into marketing text so search engines take note of the important phrases. Your writing must be convincing to both website visitors the search engines.

Your page headline should grab your reader's attention and contain keywords. Body text should stimulate interest and assure your reader they are in the right place. Are you clearly addressing the *burning question* that your ideal buyer will have? Write in a customer focused style.

Your most important keyword phrase should be used a minimum of 3 times.

1. Once in the main headline (H1)
2. Once in the first paragraph
3. Once in text that will be hyperlinked to another relevant page on your site

If you have a secondary keyword, it should be used 1-2 times.

Try and use your keywords in the beginning of the page headline. The keywords that you are targeting should appear at the beginning of your page, beginning of your paragraphs and even the beginning of your sentences. These first words are given more importance by the search engines.

Emphasize keyword phrases by putting them in **bold**, *italics* and bulleted lists.

An optimized web page should have a minimum of 300 words of text. 400 are better. Break up your content into small articles for easy reading the way a newspaper does.

The ABCs of writing your home page

The Home Page is the most important page in your website. It is the page that first greets visitors. A visitor will spend only seconds scanning your Home Page and then decide to either enter your site or leave. Your Home Page is also the most valued page by the search engines as they look for keywords.

A visitor comes to your site with an assortment of questions, but they all boil down to- "Can you help me with my problem?" This means when writing to your customer, you need to address *their* concerns and talk about solutions, not your product or service.

What are the **Advantages**, **Benefits**, and **Conveniences** (ABC's) of using your product or service? This is the heart of what a home page needs to say.

1. **Advantages**- What advantages do your product or service offer over your competition? Advantages are the ways in which you are superior in what you offer to the rest of the market. This could be largest selection in the industry or best cell phone coverage area in the nation.

2. **Benefits**- How will your product help your customer? This is entirely from the customer's perspective. Example- Save hundreds of dollars a year by using our product.

3. **Convenience**- How do you make things easier for your customer? This is something that adds comfort, is less complicated, simpler or removes work. Example: Order from the comfort of your home computer.

Build trust with your About Us page

People want to know who is running the website, how long you've been in business and how the company started.

Visitors will also look to see if you are a real company with a physical address. Tell them a little about your company. Instead of including a long history of your company, simply state when your company was founded and how long you have been serving your industry.

This is your chance to cement a relationship and connect with someone who is curious about your business. Describe how you are different and better than your competition. Share your company philosophies, awards and certifications. If you have important affiliations, this is the page to include them.

The About Us page should be concise and easy to read. Its main purpose is to build trust and credibility with your visitor. People want to feel safe and secure before they buy from you or even give you their email address.

Do you have writers block?

Many business owners are great sales people and can speak for hours to customers that are interested in what they have to offer. These same people suffer complete writers block when they sit down in front of a blank computer screen to write content for their website.

Start by jotting down a series of questions that need to be answered for each page of the website. Get someone to play the part of the customer and ask you these questions and record your conversation.

GoToMeeting.com or FreeConferenceCall.com allows you to record. You can use a transcription service to convert your words to text or send your recording to a professional writer to turn your words into your website.

This method captures your vision and passion for your business into your website. The challenge now becomes how to limit the volume of information to include onto each page.

Set up a writing schedule

Writing the content for your website can be an overwhelming project. This has been the biggest single delay in getting a website completed when business owners elect to write the content themselves.

If you are in doubt that you will have the time or the discipline to write the content for your website, then hire a professional writer.

Start with your home page. This is normally written as 4-6 short articles that introduce visitors to other areas of your website. (See the wireframe example).

The web designer will need this text as they design your website.

The next page to write is the About Us page. This is usually an easier page to write. Each page you write will be easier than the page before.

Then setup a writing schedule such as 2-5 pages per week until the writing is complete.

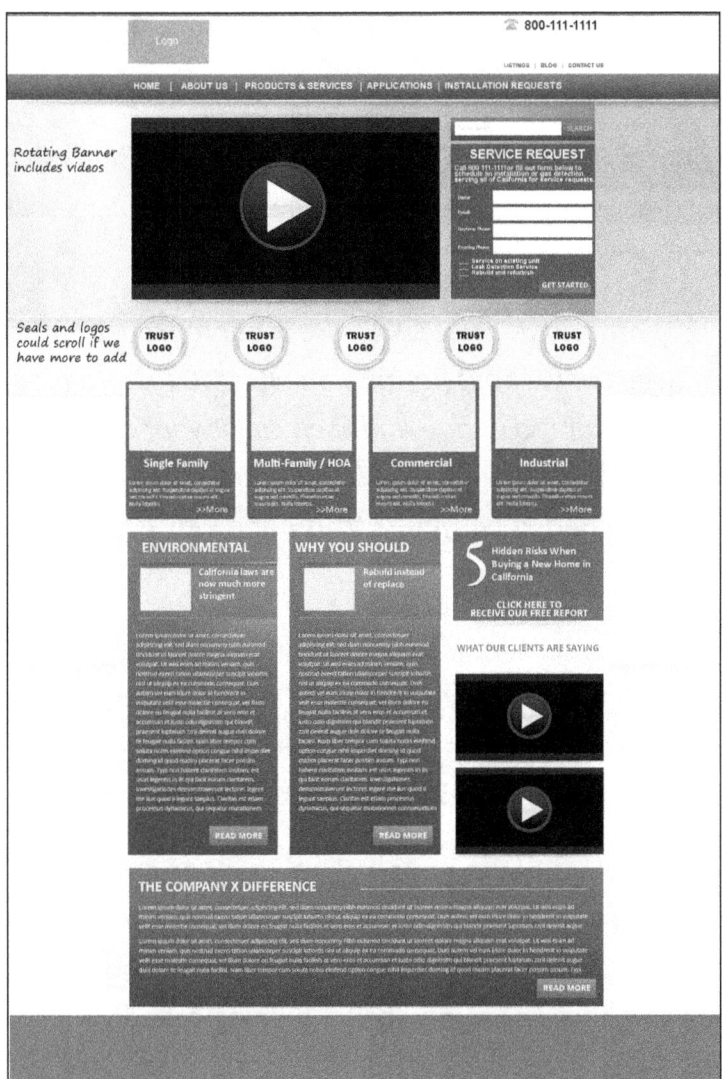

Figure 7.1 Home Page Wireframe example

Images and videos

Images should be used in every web page to add visual variety and to help communicate your ideas. Many people are visual learners and use of photos and graphics helps communicate your ideas.

Use photos you have taken, graphics you have had created or purchase royalty free stock images from services such as gettyimages.com or canstockphoto.com.

Warning- It is not OK to use a photo from another website without permission. It is NOT OK to modify a copyrighted image and then call it your own. Modifying a work, say by cropping, coloring, distorting, enlarging, etc. is not a way around Copyright laws.

It is OK to use someone's concept and create your own original image as long as no part of the original is directly copied. Merely using an original work as a model or inspiration does not by itself constitute an infringement.

Adding short videos to your website adds another dimension to your content. Videos catch a visitor's attention and persuade them to take action. They add a voice and a face to your website, helping brand you as the expert. Adding video is almost like sitting across the table from an interested prospect.

Most visitors will take the time to watch a video if the website seems relevant to their search. If you choose your videos well you will notice that people will stay on your website longer.

Web video is a powerful way to educate while allowing visitors to feel entertained. People learn in different ways and presenting only text may work well for search engines, but it limits your ability to interact with your audience. People today respond more to video than they do to text alone.

Chapter Summary

Writing for the web is different than writing for print. Writing content for your website is brief and to the point with shorter paragraphs, shorter sentences and fewer words.

Your message should connect with your targeted buyer. Address the specific needs of that customer and how you will solve a problem of directly benefit them.

The home page is the most important page in your website. What are the Advantages, Benefits, and Conveniences (ABC's) of using your product or service?

The About Us page is important in building trust. Tell them a little about your company. Describe how you are different and better than your competition. Share your company philosophies, awards and certifications.

Website Planning Steps

- ☐ Write the content for your Home Page

- ☐ Write the content for your About Us page.

- ☐ Set a schedule to write the remainder of your website.

8 You Must Design For Mobile

A good mobile strategy is important for your business. To plan your strategy you need to have a clear understanding of what your mobile visitors are looking for. The volume of mobile visitors has been growing quickly. But how significant is this to your business?

One recent study places this at 29% for the average website (2014) with a rate of growth at 30% over 2013.[8] In this study mobile numbers included mobile phones and tablets.

One finding of this study showed that websites who marketed to consumers (B2C) averaged 31% mobile visitors, while those marketing to businesses (B2B) averaged only 12% mobile traffic.

Let's look at some other recent mobile web statistics

In the US, 67% of mobile Internet users said they mostly or only used mobile, as opposed to the desktop, to go online and surf the web.[9]

45 percent of users between 18 and 29 use mobile search daily[10]

Websites marketing to consumers see 150% more traffic from mobile than websites marketing to businesses.[8]

More than half (55%) of conversions from mobile search take place within the hour, while 81% of conversions occur within five hours.[11]

Mobile search is more common in the evenings, with 22% of searches taking place between 8pm and midnight.[11]

95% of mobile users use their devices for local search.[12]

52% of all local searches are done from a mobile device.[12]

What conclusions can you draw?

1. If you have a local business that caters to consumers like a restaurant or a medical office, then your website MUST be setup for mobile visitors.

2. If your websites markets to business on a national basis, the volume from mobile is presently low, but will continue to grow. Your need is not as urgent.

3. If your website targets a younger demographic such as under 30, mobile will be important to you.

The mobile web

Mobile devices load websites more slowly than a desktop. They typically run on slower networks, mobile browsers parse and execute HTML more slowly. Mobile browser cache is smaller than desktop computers.

Page Load- This means load time is critical for your mobile version of your website if you want your visitors to have a great user experience.

You get faster load times by using fewer graphics and the ones you do use must be reduced size graphics. The website should be built to send fewer HTTP requests and the scripts should be optimized for faster execution.

 *Check your website to see how fast the page load speed is for both desktop and mobile by going to- http://developers.google.com/speed/pagespeed/insights/*

Simpler- Look at ways to greatly simplify your design, your content and the number of pages. Focus your content on just what your mobile web visitor needs to know. You want the website to be easily read when it first loads without needing to zoom in.

The numbers and sizes of mobile displays continue to grow in number. Websites today need to display correctly on smartphones (portrait and landscape); mini tablets such as the iPad mini (portrait and landscape); full size tablets such as the standard iPad (portrait and landscape) and desktop displays.

Separate Mobile Websites

For the last five years or so, the solution was to build one or more mobile versions of your website. A switcher script "sensed" which display a visitor was using and then presented the correctly sized website. This is termed adaptive websites.

Usually simplified content was presented that was shorter and there were fewer pages. Typically there are just two versions; the desktop version and the smartphone version. Many sites are still using this system today.

Figure 8.1 Adaptive Websites

The advantage of a separate mobile website is that it can be added to a current website as an add-on. These separate mobile websites can be highly optimized for page load speed.

You have the option to have different amounts of content on different versions of the websites. You can have 25-50 word pages on your mobile version and 150 words per web page if you create a separate Kindle version. And 300 words of text on a Desktop version.

This means you can completely manage the user experience

The disadvantage is that a separate website must be built and maintained for each display you want to display correctly on. This can create a real headache and extra expense when you have to manage multiple versions of the same website.

Let's say you have a desktop and a smartphone version. What to you use on a mini tablet or a full size tablet? The trend is toward an increasing number of screen sizes as the line between smartphones, tablets and desktops continues to blur. Things were simpler when there were just smartphones.

Responsive Websites

Responsive websites have the ability to detect the viewer's screen size and serve up appropriately organized text and graphics that are properly sized to ensure the best possible viewing experience.

With a responsive web design you don't have a separate mobile website. Instead you have one website that responds, re-sizes and reconfigures itself according to the viewing screen. This seems to be where the future and the direction web design and websites are headed. (See example below)

Figure 8.2 Responsive Websites

The advantage is that they are easier to deploy and maintain a single website and the responsive technology takes care of the formatting which provides a website that can be viewed well from any possible device.

Disadvantages include slower page load times. Most responsive sites present the same content on all devices, but you can hide content on mobile phones if setup that way. You are not able manage the user experience quite as well.

Which is better Responsive or Separate Mobile Websites?

So which is better for a small business? Our belief is that managing multiple website with the separate mobile websites is a cost and management time that most small businesses cannot afford.

Creating and managing separate versions of the same website can create a better visitor experience. Whether it's worth that extra expense is something each business needs to answer based on their priorities.

You might ask which works better for SEO with Google. They support either approach and this should not affect your decision. Google does not favor any particular URL format as long as they are all accessible for all Googlebots.[13]

Plan for your mobile visitor first

When you design using responsive web design, start by first considering the mobile visitor instead of the desktop visitor. This is a complete paradigm shift from our past.

By planning what your priorities are for your mobile visitor first, your design can be integrated into your desktop design.

This could be click to call on phone numbers, click to map on addresses, prioritizing the content to what mobile visitors are most interested in.

Low priority content can be hidden that can be accessed with a click.

Chapter Summary

Page load speed is very important for mobile. Mobile devices load websites more slowly than a desktop. They typically run on slower networks, mobile browsers parse and execute HTML more slowly. Mobile browser cache is smaller than desktop computers.

There are two approaches for setting up a mobile website for your business.

1. The older technology uses separate versions of your website. A switcher script "senses" which

display type a visitor has and then presents the correctly sized website.

2. The newer technology is called responsive. Responsive websites have the ability to detect the viewer's screen size and serve up appropriately organized text and graphics that are properly sized to ensure the best possible viewing experience. This is all based on a single website.

Plan how mobile visitors will interact with your website, add features that will help them such as clickable phone numbers. You can prioritize text and display high priority text only for mobile phone users.

Website Planning Steps

- ☐ Decide if you will have separate mobile websites or use a responsive web design.

- ☐ Which features are your priorities for your mobile visitor?

- ☐ Decide if mobile phone users will see all text content or only high priority content.

9 Getting Your Website Built

You are now ready to get your website built. Up until now you have been planning how your website will market for your business. Now it is time to bring in the technical experts that will design and code your new website.

In this chapter we will talk about how to select a web development firm, the typical website building process and the final QA check that you need to be run before your new site goes live.

Roles of the website project team

Before you outsource the website, you need to assess the skills and strengths of your project team.

You have the sole responsibility of getting the website built. You need to make sure these roles are being filled with either internal team members or are being outsourced. This team may or may not already exist on the same team as the web developer. Often your content writers and web strategist are hired separately.

Strategist- This person plans the purpose of the website, what products and services are being marketed to the target audience, and how the buying decision is made. They compare the competition and craft the central message for the website. They establish the goals for the website, call to actions on the website.

Figure 9.1 Anatomy of a Website Project

Project Manager- They keep the project on track and on schedule. They have the overall responsibility for the successful planning, execution, monitoring and control of the project. They manage all the moving parts and continually steer the team toward completing the website. Without a good project manager, website projects always seem to stall.

SEO Specialist- Your website needs to attract interested visitors. A skilled search engine optimization person will pick the right keywords, advise on website structure, do page optimization, establish link popularity strategies and set-up metrics to measure success. The SEO person will work closely with the content writer.

Content Writer- The writer is responsible for creating all the website content. The writer takes the message and crafts interesting and exciting text, weaving in the keywords keeping the audience and search engines interested in the website. Creative writing will create the emotional spark that causes visitors to take action.

Site Architect- They organize and categorize the website structure and content. They create the sitemap and wireframes. They work with the strategist to organize the pages into a selling sequence. They are responsible for usability and shape the user experience as they interact with the website.

Graphic Designer- The designer is responsible for the visual appearance with designs that encourage visitors to take action. The design establishes trust and credibility and is more than just "pretty." A good designer is an artist, understands visitor interaction and is a good marketer.

They will design for usability to insure a good visitor experience. Sometimes the usability expert will be a separate role in major websites.

Developer / Programmer- This person codes the website and adds the interaction functionality to the website. They turn designs into an interactive user experience. Programmers add custom database applications programs that allow your site to sell products and interact with the web visitor.

Many times one person on the team will fill multiple positions. For very large projects, each role may be filled by a team of specialists.

Before hiring a web developer, take an inventory of the skill sets that exist in your project team and where you need outside expertise. This will help you decide what skills the web developer needs to bring to the project.

Selecting a developer

Here are things to look at when you hire a web designer.

1. **Do they understand your goals?** Your website needs to meet your business objective which is why you prepared your design brief. Do they understand your goals and how they will implement them? Do they example of similar websites that they have designed and built?

2. **Which platform do they specialize in?** This is the content management / website management system used to build your website on. WordPress is the most common one in use today and is easy to take your website to another web company if you have to. Stay away from proprietary systems that don't give you the portability in case you need to move it.

   Let me give you an example of a proprietary platform. When I had my own web design firm, we developed our own content management system that allowed us to quickly deploy photo galleries, blogs and all sorts of great functionality on websites we built. The downside was it was our system and other developers couldn't easily work on the system.

   Today, I strongly recommend WordPress. This is the most popular platform in the world. It is extremely easy to find someone to work on your WordPress website.

3. **How do they design for mobile?** Do they offer responsive web design? Look at examples of their sites on your phone and tablet. Make sure their skills will match you mobile objectives.

4. **Do they understand how to design for web traffic?** Organic search rankings are important. Make sure to choose a designer experienced in SEO. They should be able to demonstrate SEO results. Search Engine

Optimization should be designed in with keywords built into navigation, page names, links and body text.

5. **Can they integrate web applications?** Most websites today includes web applications. By adding online tools, searchable databases of your work, pricing wizards, shopping carts and complex sign-up applications you can automate your business website. These can be programmed from scratch or be easily integrated with plugins which is a WordPress term.

6. **Who will maintain the website?** Once the website is complete, who will maintain the website? Website maintenance includes changing content, photos, adding pages, adding applications or adding a blog. If something breaks, who will fix it?

7. **Who will host the website?** It is nice to have one source for your web needs. Make sure you are getting high quality business website hosting that is maintained within a data center. One that has multiple Internet trunks and power backups. Stay away from designers who host on a computer in their office or apartment.

Other things to look for: What is their lead time? Will they supply a written fixed price proposal? How long have they been in business? Will they still be in business when you need help? Are they easy to reach and communicate with?

It will really come down to who are you the most comfortable in working with. Which firm will most likely deliver a website that will get you the results you need.

A website that doesn't deliver results is just an expense. A website that delivers leads or online sales is an effective marketing tool that generates revenue.

Typical Website Development Process

Each company may vary slightly in how they build out your website, but this is the typical process that most established firms follow.

1. **Information gathering-** Much of this information will already be in the design brief you created. Includes the project definition, deliverables, your design preferences, home page layout, sitemap, gathering logins, sources for images, videos and web content.

2. **Design concept-** If you have not prepared the wireframe for the home page, this will be their first step. Then one or more design concepts are done and submitted to you for approval. These are designed in a graphics program such as Photoshop or similar program. Changes are easy to make.

3. **Website Development-** Once there are approved design concepts for the home and interior pages, the design is "sliced" and coded into the platform such as WordPress.

Navigation is created and blank pages created. This is the backbone for the new website. Website functionality such as blog, photo galleries, events calendars and ecommerce are added.

4. **Page Population-** The text content, images and videos are added to the website. They are arranged on the pages to make them visually appealing. SEO is applied using the SEO plan that you prepared. If you have an ecommerce shopping cart, the products must be either manually copied over or imported into the new shopping cart.

5. **Testing and Final QA-** The developer will go through and test to make sure all of the functions on the website work correctly, the ages display correctly in the most popular browsers and on mobile displays. The website is checked for broken links, etc.

6. **Client Acceptance-** The client tests the website and verifies everything is working correctly and buys off on the website. The next section provides some guidelines and tools for your testing. You will want to prepare final list of items to fix before you accept the website.

7. **GoLive and Training-** This is the cutover to make the website live. Check to make sure emails and web forms work correctly. Do an actual transaction if your site includes ecommerce and make sure payments are

received. Verify 301 redirects have been created to make sure you don't lose your current search rankings.

Training is normally provided on using your new website. Sometimes this is done with instructional videos.

How to Quality Check Your New Website

When you are asked to buy off on your website before going live, what should you be checking for? Here are a series of visual checks and free web tools to do your own quality check.

These tests cover the basics. There are an almost overwhelming number of tools and tests that could be run. The key is to quickly uncover the major issues before you take possession of your new site. Some of these tests may need to be run once your new website is live such as the www vs. non-www check.

1. Visual checks- Go through each page on your website to make sure it displays correctly. You should check using the latest version of each major browser.

    As of the writing of this book, Chrome had a 58% browser market share, followed by Firefox with 25%. Check current browser market shares at- http://www.w3schools.com/browsers/browsers_stats.asp

An easy way to check a page using multiple browsers is with https://browsershots.org/

Test your website on your mobile phone and on an iPad. You can also use an emulator that will show how your website looks on many different display types. http://deviceponsive.com/

2. Manually test every function. Buy something from your store and sign-up for your newsletter. Do you receive all the proper email notifications? Are the email notifications formatted and worded correctly.

3. www vs. non-www- Your website should show a redirect to either the www or non-www version of your site. Do this by trying to manually switch from www.yourdomain.com to http://yourdomain.com. Does automatically switch back to the version you want?

4. Broken Links- Check all internal and external links using a broken link checker. Two free checkers that you can download and install on your computer for doing this are-

Screaming Frog SEO Spider
http://www.screamingfrog.co.uk/seo-spider/

Xenu's Link Sleuth http://xenus-link-sleuth.en.softonic.com/

5. HTML Code Validation- Verify your pages were built within coding standards. Validate all HTML code with W3C Validation. This helps with cross browser compatibility. http://validator.w3.org/

6. Website Review Software- Looking for a system that will perform a whole range of checks (not the visual or manual testing)? Try www.woorank.com.

301 redirects to prevent loss of search rankings

Many times new websites have completely new page URLs. You may be switching from pages that end in .html to pages that end in PHP. The trouble with this is you will instantly lose your search engine traffic to these pages as the search engines detect the old pages are gone. Instead put in place 301 redirects to redirect traffic to the new pages.

This can be done through your web developer where they do this in the HTaccess file. This can easily be done in Wordpress websites using a plugin called Redirection to manage 301 redirects and detect 404 errors.

Chapter Summary

Before hiring a web developer, take an inventory of the skill sets that exist in your project team and where you need outside expertise. This will help you decide what skills the web developer needs to bring to the project.

Ask questions such as what platform do they specialize in? How do they design for mobile? Do they understand how to design for web traffic? Will they help you maintain the site after it goes live? Who will host your website?

Typical Website Development Process

1. Information Gathering
2. Design Concept
3. Website Development
4. Page Population
5. Testing and Final QA
6. Client Acceptance
7. GoLive and Training

In producing a new website, you often change web page URLs. This can cause a catastrophic loss of search traffic. Put in place 301 redirects to redirect traffic to the new pages.

_____

Website Planning Steps

- ☐ Hire a Web Designer / Developer.

- ☐ Buy off on design concepts

- ☐ Do final testing before site going live.

10 Traffic Strategies 101

A constant stream of visitors is the lifeblood of any website. No matter how nice a website looks or how well it can convert a visitor into a buyer, it is utterly useless without people to view it. Before you have a site built, decide how you are going to promote it to bring in visitors.

What is the best way to get traffic to your website? The answer is simple; you need MULTIPLE sources for traffic. What works and doesn't work is always changing so you shouldn't depend on one source.

18 Ways to get website traffic

1. Organic SEO- Organic SEO means getting your website listed in the natural search results (not the paid ads). This should be your backbone strategy that attracts your best buyers when they search on Google and other search engines.

2. Local Search- This uses organic SEO methods mixed with city, state and zip codes. These "geo modifiers" bring in searchers looking for local businesses.

Figure 10.1 Sources for Website Traffic

3. Pay Per Click- Advertise directly on the search engines to get almost instant results. For the best conversions, traffic should be directed to landing pages.

4. Social Media- This includes blog marketing, social networking and more. You can set up profiles on popular social networking sites like LinkedIn, Facebook, Twitter, etc.

5. Answer questions on Yahoo Answers or askpedia.com or wiki.answers.com. This gives you a chance to answer questions related to products / services that you provide and attract new customers.

6. Encourage Bookmarking- Digg, Reddit, Stumbleupon, and Delicious are highly authoritative bookmarking sites which can dramatically improve search engine rankings if used properly. Add plugins to your blog that allow easy bookmarking by visitors.

7. Web Directories- Submitting your site to directories is still a valid and cost effective link building method that should be part of developing your portfolio of back links. Select directories that people will actually use; there are many low quality directories. The single best directory to submit to is Dmoz.org (and it's free).

8. Post Articles- Write and publish educational articles and place them on article syndication sites. Articles should be original and interesting to be successful. The articles have to be good quality.

9. Start a blog- Add a blog to your website and post at least monthly. Weekly is even better. Each blog posting

adds one new page of keyword rich content to your website. Content growth is an important part of SEO with the Google algorithm.

10. Become guest author- Write postings on other blogs. Many of the major blogs are on the lookout for quality fresh content for their site.

11. Email marketing- Develop opt-in mailing lists and market your site. Find other related companies that have prominent newsletters. Approach them to allow you to advertise in their email newsletters.

12. Promote in print ads- Include your URL on all newspaper and magazine ads.

13. Educate- Setup a webinar and promote it on the social networks. Give away a free report or analysis. Offer a free ebook on your site. This could be information that would be helpful to your visitors that contains your business information, too.

14. Traditional Marketing- Drive traffic to your site by including your website URL in all your other marketing methods such as business cards, brochures, flyers, email signatures, radio and TV ads, direct mail, etc. You get more results when you get all your marketing methods to work together.

15. Word of mouth- Tell your friends, attend networking events, become a speaker and always give out your website address. Do it both verbally and of course on your business cards.

16. Comment on Blogs- One of the best promotional strategies you can have for your website is making perceptive comments on other blogs. Posting relevant comments on related blogs is like chatting at a networking event. By visiting related blogs and engaging others, you are networking with your peers.

17. Start an affiliate program- Other websites will send you traffic if you will pay a commission when a sell is made. This is method of revenue sharing with the most common being a pay per sale model.

18. News stories- Do something newsworthy or befriend a local business reporter. Good press in a newspaper or trade publication can catch the attention of a prospective client.

Organic Search Engine Optimization

Organic SEO means getting your website listed in the natural search results (not the paid ads). Google is the most important search engine to focus on since they have the largest market share of searches.

The first step in SEO is selecting your keyword phrases. Not just any keywords, you need keyword phrases that attract buyers.

Buyers will typically use phrases with 3-5 words or sometimes longer. Buyer phrases are very specific and will include things like make and model or specific locations or details as searches get refined.

More specific keyword phrases almost always have fewer competitors and it is much faster to get top rankings. A person looking for new furniture is more likely to type in "leather sofa" rather than "leather sofas"

People search for local services with a city or state. If you are a general dentist in Portland, Oregon, don't target "Oregon dentist" if you only have an office in Portland. People will only travel a few miles to a dentist from where they work or live. Phrases that are too narrow won't deliver enough traffic. You need to find the right balance for your market.

SEO Plan

In Chapter 6, you created your sitemap and SEO Plan so the developer could build the SEO into your website. Your SEO plan should include the following-

1. Navigation Level (see Ch 6)
2. Page name to display on the menu (see Ch 6)

3. Primary keyword phrase (see Ch 6))
4. Secondary keyword
5. Title Tag
6. META Description
7. H1 Tag (main page headlines)

Each page of the website will need a primary keyword and a secondary keyword. The primary keyword is the primary focus of the web page. Choose a secondary keyword that will be used in the content writing, just to a lesser extent.

If the website is a local business, the secondary phrase should be the City, State to help apply local SEO.

Title Tag Best Practices

The Title Tag describes a webpage for both search engines and for visitors. It is the single most important SEO element for page level SEO (on-page factors). Many times simply fixing Title Tags alone will improve search engine rankings for a website.

It not only appears visibly at the top of your browser, it appears in the HTML code of your website and as the main headline in the search engine results page (SERP).

A well-crafted title tag will help get a top ranking and catch the attention of a searcher to begin the conversion process by inviting them to your web page. It should be an accurate, concise description of the content on the web page.

Title Tag format- Keyword 1, Keyword 2 | Company (or brand) name

Your Title Tag should be unique (not duplicated on other pages). It should contain the central topic of the web page. Words placed at the beginning of the Title Tag are given more importance than the words at the end. This is why the most important keyword phrase for a web page should be at the beginning. The company name is typically placed at the end.

An alternate approach- If you company brand is strong and people will search for you by your brand, then place the company name or brand name first and follow it with the keyword phrases.

Title Tag length- Less than 65-70 characters

This is because 70 characters is the maximum length Google will display on the SERP. Title tags can be longer, the search engines will just cut off the Title Tag and indicate that it was cut off with an ellipsis(...) Remember that the words placed at the beginning are given more weight by the search engines so longer tags don't make sense. 65-70 characters usually give you room for two keyword phrases and the company name.

Local- If yours is a local business seeking local customers, then include city and or state. Typically people will search using the company name + location or company type + location.

Compelling- Your Title Tag will appear in the search results. Make it compelling so it will pull in more visits from the search results.

Unique- Each page should have a unique Title Tag. Duplicate titles will harm search rankings.

META Description Tags Best Practices

META Description tags are not about SEO directly, but their message will attract guests to your website. Description Tags are used as the description in Google search results; so make them compelling. They should be unique and relevant for each page on your website.

On a search results page the Title Tag serves as the title for the search result. The META Description serves as the body. When no Description Tag exists, a snippet of relevant text is pulled from the page text.

Think of your Description Tag as a mini elevator pitch that is done in 160 characters or less. So its length is not much longer than a tweet.

Competition- Look at your competition before you start writing. Get an idea of their messages. You want to stand out and be better than they are.

Unique and relevant- Every page should have its own description that accurately describes that page. Make them compelling mini ads that accurately describe that page. This helps draw in targeted visitors.

Advertising Copy- The purpose of the META Description is to encourage people to click on the search engine result and come to your web page. Include a call to action to entice people to click through to your site. One technique is to include your phone number to encourage phone calls. Some people will call directly off the results page without clicking through to the site.

Keywords Unnecessary- Descriptions do not affect rankings. You do not need to worry about using keywords within your Description Tags. Titles should be crafted to entice people to click on your search result. Descriptions are more about conversion rather than SEO.

Length- Search engines will only display up to 160 characters. The optimal length of a description is 150-160 characters.

H1 Header Tag Best Practices

H1 Tags are the main web page headline. They should contain your most important keyword phrase and grab an arriving visitor's interest. Failing to use any H1 heading tags is a common SEO mistake. Many sites that have H1 headings, waste this important real estate with a very prominent WELCOME showing on their home page.

Headings are defined with the "<h1>" to "<h6>" tags. The H1 Header is the largest and the most important of these tags. Search engines put the most weight in H1 heading and it is regarded as the most important visible text on the web page.

Header Tag Optimization Tips

1. The main topic of the page should be the H1. Use H2 tags to break down the main topic into sub topics.

2. H1 tags should include the primary keyword phrase for the page. Additional keywords can be placed in the H2 tags. H3 tags carry only a minor importance with the search engines, so use sparingly with keywords.

3. Don't overuse the H1 and H2 tags. Each page should have only one H1 and one or two H2 tags. H4 thru H6 don't carry any real SEO weight.

4. Limit the length of each tag to a phrase or simple sentence. This is the same logic you would apply to any article headline.

5. Do not repeat keywords in these tags, as that will be flagged as spam. Avoid stuffing keywords in heading tags.

6. Words at the front of the heading tags are more important to the search engines.

7. On eCommerce product pages, the product name is generally what you are optimizing for and this should be placed in the H1 tag.

8. For blog posts, the posting title should be used within the H1 tags.

How to Use Keywords

Use your keywords visibly on each web page for maximum benefit. Building these keywords into every facet of your website forms the messaging that allows you to better connect with your prospect.

1. Page URLs- Name pages with keywords phrases that describe the page. Separate keywords with hyphens.

2. Navigation- The navigation should be SEO friendly HTML links rather than JavaScript links or an image map. Use keywords as much as possible in the navigation links.

3. Breadcrumbs- These are a trail left so visitors will know their location. **Example: Home page > Product One > Installation Instructions.** Use breadcrumb navigation on larger sites that include keywords.

4. Title Tags- Each page should have unique Title tag. Keyword phrases should be at the beginning and the company name should be at the end.

5. Description and Keywords Tags- Use unique page descriptions and keywords tags for each page that accurately describes each web page.

6. H1/H2 Tags- H1 Tags are the main web page headline. They should contain your most important keyword phrase and grab an arriving visitor's interest. Additional keywords can be placed in the H2 tags.

7. Body Text- This is the page content. Each page of your website should have 250 or more words of text. Each page should include your most important keywords and if yours is a local business, your pages should show the cities that you serve.

8. Emphasized text- Within the content, use keywords in bold and italicized text, in bulleted lists and numbered lists. This makes them standout as important.

9. Internal Links- link to relevant internal pages using your keywords.

10. Images- Name images with your keyword phrase and use them in your ALT text.

Pay Per Click Advertising

Pay-per-click marketing is a way to quickly get your offer in front of millions of people. This is where you only pay when someone clicks on your ad. Examples are Google AdWords, Facebook ads, etc.

PPC can get great results fast or cause you to burn through a lot of money and get no results. The difference is in the planning and execution of your campaign. Here are some tips to maximize your PPC marketing efforts.

1. Keywords- Choose your keywords carefully. They should be highly relevant to your product or service. Don't just select popular phrases. **Longer phrases are better for getting PPC results.** Research shows that people just starting to learn about a subject will search using 1-2 word phrases. People ready to purchase or take action will search using specific 3-5 word phrases.

2. Ad Copy- Your ad is your initial entry to your landing page. It should include the specific keyword phrase the searcher used to find your ad. This means having a different ad for each keyword phrase (or group of keyword phrases) will increase your conversion rate.

3. Use landing pages- Never send PPC traffic to the home page of your website. A landing page is a simplified web page with limited or no navigation links and is focused on getting your visitor to take a specific action. To

maximize conversion, the keyword phrase used in the original search, should be used in the ad, in the landing page name and headline of the landing page.

4. Landing page headlines- The landing page headline should be located in the top left portion of the page just below a small company logo. It should include your keyword phrase and clearly state a compelling benefit or how you solve your visitor's problem.

5. Call to action- Make it easy for your visitor to take action on your landing page. Locate your embedded form or action link where it is clearly visible and above the fold.

Use Social Media Optimization

Social Media Optimization or SMO is a form of word of mouth marketing through the use of social networking, social bookmarking, blogging and media sharing (photo, video) websites. The focus of SMO is on relationship and trust building. SMO is about increasing traffic flow to your social media content pages.

SMO focuses on securing traffic from sources other than search engines. When your content is placed on your website such as with a blog, traffic flow will increase to the website.

SMO is giving people a reason to visit and link to your site because of great original content. Links from social media back to your site are important for SEO. Improved search rankings are often a benefit of successful SMO.

Social media marketing is very different than traditional marketing. It's about publishing interesting content, creating relationships and trust. It's not about selling, though people do prefer to buy from those they know and trust.

Use social media to build your brand and your reputation, not to sell products. Brand yourself as a leader. Your brand is what you represent, what you care about and your connection to others. You want to be the unique and persuasive voice in your market. Your goal is to create a cultural following.

Social media participants can interact with you and learn your products or services in the process. Social media focuses on sharing content using RSS feeds, social news and sharing buttons, user rating and polling tools, and incorporating third-party community functionalities like images and videos. Sharing is made easy by adding social media sharing and bookmarking buttons along with your content.

Combine SMO with your SEO efforts. Use it to bring traffic to your website through links and gain better search engine rankings.

Chapter Summary

What is the best way to get traffic to your website? The answer is simple; you need MULTIPLE sources for traffic.

Organic SEO means getting your website listed in the natural search results (not the paid ads). This should be your backbone strategy that attracts your best buyers when they search on Google and other search engines. Use your keywords visibly on each web page for maximum benefit.

Pay-per-click marketing is a way to quickly get your offer in front of millions of people. PPC can get great results fast or cause you to burn through a lot of money and get no results. The difference is in the planning and execution of your campaign.

Social media optimization or SMO is a form of word of mouth marketing through the use of social networking, social bookmarking, blogging and media sharing (photo, video) websites. The focus of SMO is on relationship and trust building. SMO is about increasing traffic flow to your social media content pages.

Website Planning Steps

- ☐ Identify a minimum of 3 traffic sources for your website

- ☐ Complete your SEO Plan

- ☐ Apply SEO to each web page using Your SEO plan as your guide

11 Metrics and KPIs

Once you make your website live, you will need to set up your measurement systems. These are the metrics and key performance indicators that will track your website performance.

In business if you want to improve say, employee performance, you set goals and measure performance. You may need to meet with them weekly, to guide them toward the results you want.

The same is true with your website. You need your website to deliver results. You need to set goals and measure performance. Only in the case of your website you will continue to make adjustments and watch how performance changes. In Chapter 12 we will discuss the ongoing work and changes you can make with your website.

Websites have the advantage that there are a tremendous number of things that can be measured. What is important is to boil these down to metrics that are meaningful and that will help you reach your business goals.

You will establish the major goals and the key measurements that show movement toward these goals. These are the KPIs, or Key Performance Indicators. Each KPI will have multiple metrics that will help you focus on how to improve it.

Key Performance Indicators

Remember all KPIs are metrics, but not all metrics are KPIs. KPIs are metrics that help steer toward your business goals. A KPI is a quantifiable measure of your marketing progress. You should focus on 3-4 of the most important metrics that will provide meaning at all levels of the organization.

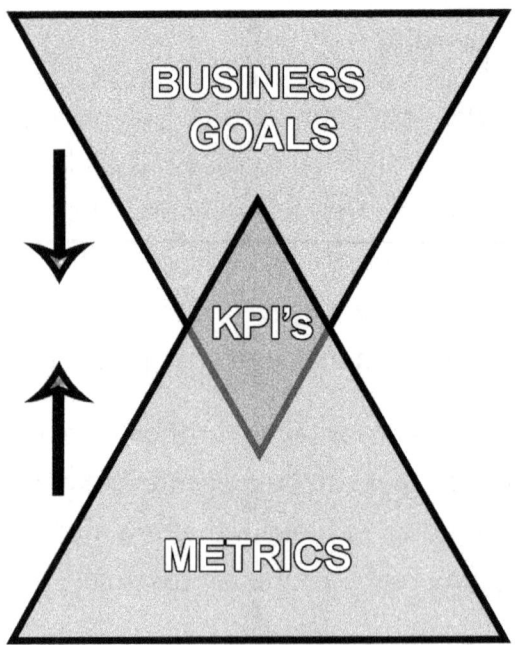

Figure 11.1 Key Performance Indicators

To select the key performance indicators for your website you need to look back at the business purpose for your website. See Chapter 1.

What makes for a good key performance indicator?

1. It should inform how the business is doing
2. Be a measure of success or failure
3. Be decided upon by management
4. Be easily understood by all levels of the organization
5. Inspire action

By using these attributes of a good KPI, visits to your website or rankings in the search engines are not good KPIs. These are metrics that don't inform how the business is doing. They are not a measure of success or failure toward meeting goals.

Visits may be a supporting metric of the KPI transactions per day, or sales $ per day. Visits are only a small piece of the puzzle. To get a transaction you need a good volume of interested visitors. They need to be interested and engage well with the site and there needs to be a good conversion rate.

Visits are not close enough to the business goal to be considered a KPI.

Lead Generation

Let's say your number one business goal was to generate new sales leads for your company through online quote requests from web form submissions and phone calls.

Using Google Analytics you can track metrics such as the numbers of visits to any particular page. You can also track actions such as web form completions. Web form completions would be the number of visits to the thank you page after the web form has been completed. Phone calls can be tracked by setting a unique phone number for the website that forwards to your main number.

Then website key performance indicators could be-

1. New leads from your website / week- This would be the total phone calls and form submissions.
2. Conversion rate- This is the total new leads divided by website visits.
3. Web form abandonment rate- This is the percent of people that go to a form and then fail to complete it. A high abandonment rate means the web form is creating a barrier to conversions.

$$\text{Formula} = \frac{\text{(WEB FORM VISITS} - \text{THANK YOU PAGE VISITS)}}{\text{WEB FORM VISITS}}$$

4. New customers acquired from the website. This could be online sales or converted leads.

5. PPC cost per lead- If you are using Google Adwords, track and reduce your $ spent divided by the number of leads.
6. Quantity and quality of online reviews. Track the number of new reviews on Google+, Yelp, Angie's list etc. You can use companies like reputology.com to monitor the review sites for you with both free and paid versions.

eCommerce Sales

Let's say your primary objective was direct sales from your website. What would some possible KPIs be for this type of website?

1. Daily or weekly sales volume. This could be total sales $, units sold or sales $ by product line.
2. Conversion rate would be the visitors who purchase divided by the total number of website visitors.
3. Shopping cart abandonment rate. Track the number of people that start, but do not complete the purchase process divided by the number that starts the purchase process.
4. PPC conversion rate. This is the number of people that complete an action divided by the total number of people that click on an ad.
5. PPC cost per sale. These are the total dollars spent divided by the number of sales.

6. Affiliate performance rate. This could be the number of leads, sales $ or conversion rate.
7. Returns rate. Dollars or units returned for a time period divided by sales volume.
8. Quantity and quality of product reviews. Use this to remove the low performers and only keep the best rated products.

These KPIs will form the dashboard that allows you to quickly gauge your success or failure of your website and how visitors are engaging with it.

Use metrics to support KPIs

Use metrics that influence a KPI to help guide what changes and improvements you should make to your website. There may be dozens of underlying metrics that guide you toward an improvement on a KPI.

Suppose your KPI was to achieve a 2% conversion rate on your lead generation website. You would setup a series of metrics that could help improve the conversion rate.

If your conversion rate was 0.5%, what would you look for?

You could start by looking at how your website visitors are engaging with your website. Do they find your content interesting?

This is where using your website analytics such as Google Analytics comes in handy. You can analyze factors that lead to conversion such as bounce rate.

Bounce Rate is the percentage of visitors that leave without moving deeper into your website. These are the people who look only at a single page and then leave. A high bounce rate often leads to a lower conversion rate.

The exception to this is if you are sending traffic to a landing page as in a PPC campaign. Typical landing pages have no easy way to navigate to other pages so they have high bounce rates and still have good conversion rates.

Typical bounce rates for informational websites are 45%-55%. Ecommerce websites are typically lower at about 25%.

Ways to improve bounce rate include-

1. Verify you are targeting the right prospects with your keywords.
2. Add clear call to actions to move them into your selling sequence.
3. Make sure your call-to-actions are compelling and highly visible.
4. Rewrite and make your content more compelling.
5. Add videos to illustrate products or services in use.
6. Reorganize content to make it less confusing.
7. Format your information into shorter paragraphs.

8. Add trust elements such as trust logos, privacy policies, returns policies, product reviews, testimonials etc.

This is just one possible metric. Other visitor engagement metrics include-

- Average time on site. This is typically 2 min or longer.
- Average pages per visit. This should be as high as possible.
- Repeat visitors. Visitors that return are more engaged.

Google Analytics and Webmaster Tools

These are two free Google products that you should setup for your website to help gather your metrics data.

Google Analytics is the single most used analytics package for websites. This allows you to measure a huge number of metrics. It allows you to track conversions, sales funnel activity, detailed engagement by page, demographics information about your visitors and much much more.

Setup is easy. There is a tremendous amount of documentation and tutorials available to help you get the most out of it. You can even design a custom report and have them emailed to you automatically. Data can be exported to Excel making analysis easy.

Google Webmaster Tools gives you valuable measurements on the SEO health of your website. It shows what is working well and provides tools that will uncover the sources of a problem. This is a free Google tool and is even more powerful when you link it with your Google Analytics account.

1. Enable Email Notifications- Under preferences you can enable email notifications. You will generally receive no more than one email a day advising you of potential issues with your website.

2. HTML Improvements- Listed under the Search Appearance section. This will advise you of technical improvements that you can make to improve your search results. This includes Title Tags, Meta Descriptions and non-indexed content.

3. Search Queries- Listed under the Search Traffic section. Track how often your website is appearing in Googles search queries (impressions) and the click volume for each search phrase. It will Display your average search position for each phrase in the Google search results.

4. Links to Your Site- Also under the Search Traffic section. This will show the number of links coming to your site, from which websites and the link text (anchor text) that is being used.

5. Manual Actions- Hopefully this section is empty. This would be where a notification of penalty is posted if someone from the web spam team has determined that your website has violated Google's webmaster guidelines.

   If a manual action was imposed, details will be listed. You should address the problems. Your website should follow Google's webmaster guidelines. From within Webmaster Tools, you can then request a review by Google for reconsideration.

6. Index Status- Listed under the Google Index section. This shows the number of URL's that Google has been able to crawl and index. It will also show the numbers of URLs blocked by a robots.txt file.

   The robots.txt file is a simple text file that defines rules for search engines to crawl and index a site. It allows a site owner to specify which robots should crawl the site and which areas of their website should be left alone.

7. Crawl Errors. Listed under the crawl section. Track the pages not found (404 errors). This allows you to view which URLs are being "not found" and then to mark them as fixed.

8. Crawl Stats. Listed under the crawl section. There are a number of measurements, but I watch the average time spent downloading a page. This gives me a relative

measure of page load speed. If this trends upward, then you may be having a page load speed problem. For a more in depth look at page load speed go to Google's Page Speed Insights.

Studies have shown that web pages that take over 2 seconds to load will quickly lose visitors, particularly those on mobile devices. One study found that 18% of shopping cart abandonment was due to slow loading pages.

9. Sitemaps- Listed under the crawl section. Make sure Google has processed your XML sitemaps. You can submit new sitemaps here and view if there are any issues with your sitemaps.

While there are many more tools and metrics that you can look at, these are the main ones I track on a weekly basis.

Other free sources for metrics

SEOQuake tool bar- This is a free add-on for your browser. This can be installed on most major browsers such a Chrome, Firefox, Opera and Safari. The Toolbar provides metrics such Alexa Rank, pages indexed by Google, Title tags, META descriptions, keyword density, text volume, etc. for a web page you navigate to.

 *Keep this plugin off until you arrive to a page you want to analyze. Then turn it on and refresh the*

page. If you leave it on, it will make too many queries and Google is likely to ban your computer from doing searches for a short time.

MajesticSEO.com- This website has some powerful link popularity analysis tools. There are free and paid options. The free version provides many excellent reports and analysis on most websites.

OpenSiteExplorer.org. This is another website that provides link popularity or backlink analysis on most any website. There are free and paid versions and these metrics are different than MajesticSEO.com.

SEMrush.com- Provides all sorts of traffic and keywords metrics. There are free and paid plans. Great source for doing an analysis of your competitors sites as well as gathering metrics on your own website.

Woorank.com- This site does an online website analysis. It will pull together over 50 different metrics and prepare a report for you. You can run one free analysis per week or purchase one of their paid plans if you are tracking multiple websites.

Baseline metrics

Once your website goes live, record baseline values for each of your metrics and KPIs. This gives you the starting point. Schedule a weekly time to record the new values for each.

An easy way to track this is to setup an Excel spreadsheet and keep adding columns for each new weekly measurement. From here you can add graphs that allow you to visually see trends.

Chapter Summary

KPIs are metrics that help steer toward your businesses goals. A KPI is a quantifiable measure of your marketing progress. You should focus on 3-4 of the most important metrics that will provide meaning at all levels of the organization.

KPIs will form the dashboard that allows you to quickly gauge either the success or failure of your website and how visitors are engaging with it. There may be dozens of underlying metrics that guide you toward improvement on a KPI.

Google Analytics and **Webmaster Tools** are two great sources for metrics. These are two free Google products that you should setup for your website to help gather your metrics data.

Other free sources for metrics include SEOQuake tool bar, MajesticSEO.com, OpenSiteExplorer.org, semrush.com and Woorank.com.

Chart KPIs and metrics on a fixed weekly schedule.

Website Planning Steps

- ☐ Identify 3-4 KPIs that will support your business goals.

- ☐ For each KPI, identify 3-5 metrics that will influence the KPI's performance.

- ☐ Setup Google Analytics and Google Webmaster tools for your website.

- ☐ Gather baseline metrics as your website goes live.

12 After Your Site Goes Live

Once your website goes live, your work has only begun. Your website is an important marketing tool that serves as a connection to your prospects and customers.

Websites must be updated; new content added regularly, changes made to improve performance of KPIs and metrics. The worst thing you can do is to get your website project completed and then set it aside and forget about it.

You need to assign the ongoing maintenance and improvement of your site to a key person in your organization. This is usually someone with marketing responsibilities.

You can outsource some of the routine work, but someone on your team must take responsibility for the oversight of your website performance.

What should your ongoing website marketing include? You need to develop your own process based on your business goals and the competitiveness of your market.

Remember the technology and competition in website marketing is always advancing. It takes a lot of time and effort to reach and maintain a leadership position on the web.

Setup a regular website review meeting to track results and agree on action plans. For most businesses, this is a formal monthly meeting.

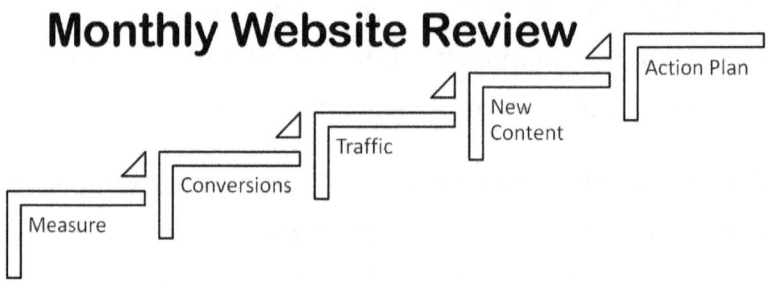

Figure 12.1 Monthly Website Review

There are seven areas that you should design your ongoing website marketing program around. Each month review your accomplishments and spend time redefining your next month's action plan.

1. Monitor and measure
2. Keep content updated
3. Improve conversions
4. Grow your traffic base
5. Grow your content
6. Add reviews and testimonials
7. Monitor your competition

Monitor and measure

Use your KPIs and metrics you defined in Chapter 11 and begin systematically recording your metrics and monitor your progression toward your goals.

You will quickly see that some of your metrics provide valuable insights that help you make improvements. Other metrics are just meaningless information.

At least monthly, evaluate if your measurements are meaningful. If they are not, prune away the ones that are not helping improve and add new ones that will.

You are creating a standard system for continual improvement of your website. This is often called the PDCA cycle used in process improvement.

Plan- Identify opportunities to create action plans for change.

Do- Make small scale changes based on your plans.

Check- Use metrics data to see if the change made a difference.

Act- If successful, keep the change and use on a wider scale. If unsuccessful, begin the cycle again.

Your website marketing will be fluid and ever changing. Use performance measurements to guide your website to get better and better results.

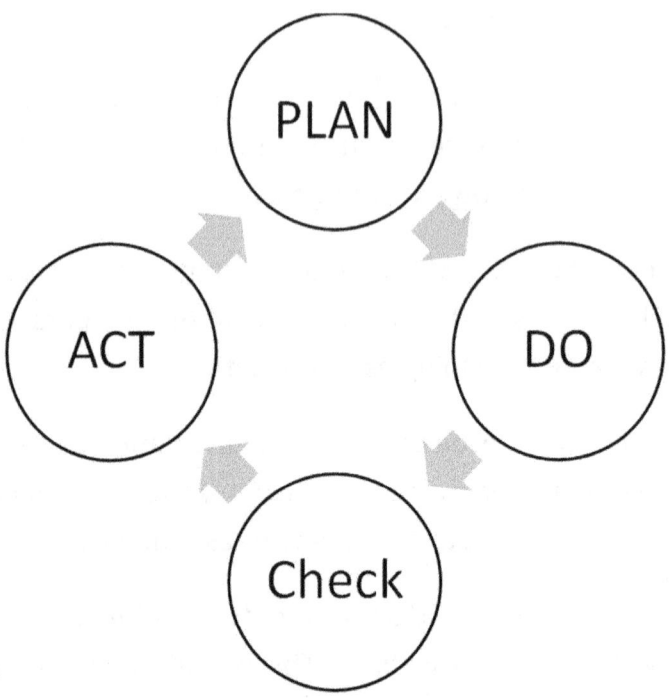

Figure 12.2 PDCA Cycle

Keep content updated

Your website should demonstrate the value your business offers to prospective clients. A stale outdated website sends the wrong message about your business.

Savvy web visitors can quickly spot old content. This is the difference between a brochure and a newspaper. Current and timely is better.

Fresh, new content helps keep visitors engaged and coming back. For ideas, monitor what your competition is doing to keep their sites fresh. Borrow the best ideas and apply to your website.

There is nothing worse than prominently posting your April special on your site when it is currently July.

Your website will have two types of content. Content that change slowly such as the About Us or FAQ pages. Then there are web pages that are likely to change regularly such as specials, products and services, meet the team and in the news pages.

Guidelines for evaluating content

- Update or remove outdated information.

- Fix spelling and grammatical errors. You can run a spell checker over your website.

- Avoid large blocks of text. Paragraphs should be brief with 1-4 sentences per paragraph.

If your website has a blog, make sure new postings are written regularly.

If your website offers specials, update and change at least monthly to encourage return visits.

Make it part of your monthly website review to identify outdated content and to replace them or update them. Constantly adding new and fresh content will help your search engine rankings.

As part of your regular website maintenance check monthly for broken links by running a scan of the site. Check for 404 errors which indicate the need to add 301 redirects. Google Webmaster Tools is a good place to check this.

At least quarterly check how your website looks with the latest browsers. Sometimes new browsers will "break" some graphic on your website. Usually this is a simple fix, but you want to keep your website looking good to your website visitors. Use a tool like browsershots.org to check a few key pages.

Improve conversions

You want to make it easy for your visitors reach to reach their objectives. This could be to buy from you or at least engage with your business. Your initial call to actions and selling sequence is only a best guess and a good starting point.

You will want to use metrics to guide you in making changes. One of your first steps is to identify and optimize your conversion funnel.

These are the steps from arriving to your website, learning about what you offer, taking action and then arriving onto your thank You page.

In Google Analytics you can identify your conversion funnel by entering the page URL of each step. You will be able to see the fall off of people as they progress through your conversion steps.

Your job is to entice and guide your visitor through your conversion process. Design and optimize your path for your best buyer. Use the information from your funnel metrics to optimize the conversion of each step.

Conversion tips

1. Make call-to-action clear and compelling
2. Show the benefits and provide proof in the form of reviews and testimonials.
3. Remove any friction points. These are points where they have to change from page to page, forms that require too much information. Your goal is to simplify.

Conversion improvement is best done by making many small changes and watching the impact of each change before moving onto the next one.

Another technique to improve conversions is called remarketing. This involves regular emailing of special offers to people who have registered on your website to receive these offers.

Typically companies will offer free shipping on the first order to a new customer if they elect to sign up to receive these email notifications of deals and offers.

You would then email your list weekly on special deals. People that arrive to your website from these emails are ready to buy. Your conversion rate and total sales increase with this technique.

Grow your traffic base

Traffic to your website will come from multiple sources. Each will behave differently. You will probably receive organic search traffic, referrals from other websites, visitors from your social media and paid advertising from each of your campaigns.

You need to look at each source in detail to understand what you may want to change.

Identify each source of traffic to your website using Google Analytics (or other analytics). Look at each source for not only how many visits there are, but also how the traffic engages with your website (bounce rate, visit duration, and number of pages per visit)

If you are looking at traffic from organic search traffic, look at which phrase are bringing the best traffic that engages well on your site. Which pages are they entering your site on? Which pages are they exiting on? Spend time with your analytics package and it will begin to tell a story of which traffic is engaging well with your site.

Make small changes and sit back and watch for improvement. Keep the changes that work.

You can keep adding new traffic channels, perhaps an affiliate program, perhaps banner advertising with some association you are a member of.

With analytics you can track the quantity and quality of the traffic and decide if it is worth investing more time or advertising dollars.

Grow your content

Content growth strategies such as adding a blog to your website is very important in today's SEO. Use blogs, press releases, articles and new product sections as ways to regularly grow your website content.

Adding a blog to your website is a powerful way to improve your website SEO and grow content. This involves a technique known as SEO Blogging. Each posting adds one more page of fresh original, keyword rich content to your website.

In SEO Blogging you use blogging to optimize your website. It requires writing interesting and original material to attract links from other bloggers. Here is how the process works.

1. Set-up a blog on your website. Place it in a folder such as mydomain.com/blog (never in a subdomain such as blog.mydomain.com). This is very important since others will link to your content and you want those links to benefit your entire website and not just your blog.

2. Keyword plan- Create a list of keywords that you want your website to rank well for. Every phrase should have a page on your website that it relates to. Place the URL of the page next to the keyword phrase that most closely relates to that phrase. For the best results you should be using these keyword phrases visibly on the content in your web pages.

3. Topic- Select a topic that interests you and that you think your readers will enjoy. The topic should be closely related to a keyword phrase from your keyword plan; this should be in line with the theme of your blog. Your blog should answer a popular question, solve a problem or entertain your audience.

4. Keyword Focused Posting- The key is to have a highly keyword focused posting that will link to a specific page on your site. Select one primary keyword phrase that you will center your entire posting around. Use the keyword in the title, in the first paragraph, at least one other time in the posting and once as a hyperlink to the most relevant page on your website.

For SEO Blogging, make it easy for readers to be able to scan through your content quickly and easily. A typical blog posting should be about 250 words and be written in a simple format.

To build an audience you should post 1-2 times per week and stay focused around your primary blog topic.

Add reviews and testimonials

Customer reviews need to be an important part of your marketing effort. These are reviews that your customers will leave on Google+, Yelp, Angie's List, etc.

These reviews provide the social proof that you are a reputable business to work with. Many of these sites will provide ratings that your prospective customers will use as part of their decision on who to buy from.

Adding reviews should be part of your marketing effort. Some companies automatically send postcards or emails along with every transaction asking for their customers to leave a review.

To manage these reviews you should monitor any new reviews that are placed on these review sites and immediately respond to any negative review and try and turn around an unhappy customer. These review sites will allow the person that submits a review to change it.

Reputation management companies help make checking review sites easy. Reputology for example can be setup to email you daily with updates from the 5 major review sites.

Provide written and video testimonials on your website. An easy way to get these testimonials is to request feedback on every transaction. Positive feedback can become testimonials.

Negative feedback can be used as a way to improve your business practices.

One very good system that I have seen sends a feedback request for every transaction. Positive feedback sends the person to a page encouraging them to leave a review on Yelp or Google+. Negative reviews are sent to a thank you page telling them that their concerns will be responded to.

Monitor your competition

Setup a system where you review your competition's websites, social media and paid advertising so you can track what they are doing.

Look at any new offerings. Set up some metrics to see if they are launching any new Internet marketing initiatives.

A few simple metrics recorded down every few months will alert you to which competitors are getting more aggressive in their marketing.

Here is a simple competitor analysis that can be done in less than 5 minutes per competitor website.

1. SEOQuake toolbar

    a. Alexa traffic ranking will indicate more website traffic going to their website.

    b. Pages indexed by Google- if this is growing, have they implemented a content growth strategy

2. SEMrush.com

    a. Search Engine Traffic shows the estimated traffic from organic search (first 2 pages of results)

    b. This source will show you if they are using PPC and what ads they are using

A simple analysis that only shows 2-3 metrics is all you need to see which competitors expanding their marketing effort.

Chapter Summary

Websites must be updated; new content added regularly, changes made to improve performance of KPIs and metrics.

There are seven areas that you should design your ongoing website marketing program around. Each month review your accomplishments and spend time redefining your next month's action plan.

1. Monitor and measure
2. Keep content updated
3. Improve conversions
4. Grow your traffic base
5. Grow your content
6. Add reviews and testimonials
7. Monitor your competition

Website Planning Steps

- ☐ Assign responsibility for someone to be in charge of managing and improving the website results.

- ☐ Setup monthly review meetings with your marketing team to review KPIs, metrics, results and action plans.

- ☐ Implement a strategy to regularly add new content to your website.

- ☐ Setup a quarterly review of your competitor websites to spot changes in their online marketing.

Website Planning Checklist

Refer to the chapter shown for more information.

- ☐ Describe why you want this new website (Ch 1)
- ☐ What are your business marketing objectives (Ch 1)
- ☐ Describe purpose and objectives for website (Ch 1)

- ☐ Describe your best buyer. (Ch 2)
- ☐ Develop buyer profiles or personas. (Ch 2)
- ☐ Do keyword research and rate for relevance. (Ch 2)
- ☐ Settle on your domain name. (Ch 3)

- ☐ Decide if you will keep or update your logo. Then get a high resolution version for your website design. (Ch 3)

- ☐ Decide what colors to use in branding. (Ch 3)

- ☐ Map out selling sequences by buyer type. (Ch 4)
- ☐ Create a prioritized list of actions for visitors. (Ch 4)
- ☐ List out ways you will reassure visitors and build trust. (Ch 4)
- ☐ Create an inventory of videos you will use. (Ch 4)
- ☐ Integrate educational marketing? (Ch 4)

- ☐ List 3-5 reference websites. Include comments of what you like and what you don't like. (Ch 5)
- ☐ List of functions and features to include. (Ch 5)

- ☐ Do a competitive traffic review and compare your website to your competition. (Ch 5)
- ☐ Create the sitemap for your website. (Ch 6)
- ☐ Create the SEO Plan for your website. (Ch 6, 10)
- ☐ Create the wireframe for your home page. (Ch 6)
- ☐ Prepare the design brief completing as much information as possible. (Ch 6)
- ☐ Write the content for your Home Page. (Ch 7)
- ☐ Write the content for your About Us page. (Ch 7)
- ☐ Set a schedule to write the remainder of your website. (Ch 7)
- ☐ Decide if you will have separate mobile websites or use a responsive web design. (Ch 8)
- ☐ Which features are your priorities for your mobile visitor? (Ch 8)
- ☐ Decide if mobile phone users will see all text content or only high priority content. (Ch 8)
- ☐ Hire a Web Designer / Developer. (Ch 9)
- ☐ Buy off on design concepts. (Ch 9)
- ☐ Do final testing before site going live. (Ch 9)
- ☐ Identify a minimum of 3 traffic sources for your website. (Ch 10)
- ☐ Complete your SEO Plan. (Ch 10)

- ☐ Apply SEO to each web page using Your SEO plan as your guide. (Ch 10)
- ☐ Identify 3-4 KPIs that will support your business goals. (Ch 11)
- ☐ For each KPI, identify 3-5 metrics that will influence KPI performance. (Ch 11)
- ☐ Setup Google Analytics and Google Webmaster tools for your website. (Ch 11)
- ☐ Gather baseline metrics as your website goes live. (Ch 11)
- ☐ Assign responsibility for someone to be in charge of managing and improving the website results. (Ch 12)
- ☐ Setup monthly review meetings with your marketing team to review KPIs, metrics, results and action plans. (Ch 12)
- ☐ Implement a strategy to regularly add new content to your website. (Ch 12)
- ☐ Setup a quarterly review of your competitor websites to spot changes in their online marketing. (Ch 12)

References and Sources

Introduction

1. *How we got from 1 to 162 million websites on the internet,* http://royal.pingdom.com/2008/04/04/how-we-got-from-1-to-162-million-websites-on-the-internet/ ,data accessed January 2013.

2. April 2014 Web Server Survey, http://news.netcraft.com/archives/2014/04/02/april-2014-web-server-survey.html , data accessed April 2014.

3. World Internet Users and Population Stats, http://www.internetworldstats.com/stats2.htm#americas , data accessed January 2013.

4. comScore Releases March 2014 U.S. Search Engine Rankings, http://www.comscore.com/Insights/Press_Releases/2014/4/comScore_Releases_March_2014_U.S._Search_Engine_Rankings , data accessed April 2014.

5. Internet Usage by US State, http://www.internetworldstats.com/unitedstates.htm , data accessed April 2014.

6. Stanford Web Credibility Research, http://credibility.stanford.edu/guidelines/index.html, Data accessed Jan 2011.

7. Web users judge sites in the blink of an eye, http://www.nature.com/news/2006/060109/full/news060109-13.html , data accessed April 2014.

8. A Study on How Much Mobile Traffic is going to Small Business Websites, http://www.dougwilliams.com/study-much-mobile-traffic-going-small-business-websites/, written by Doug Williams May 2014.

9. Post PC era in the US, http://ondeviceresearch.com/blog/post-pc-era-in-the-us-#sthash.HKJxpFZY.OnzXB1tP.dpbs, data accessed May 2014.

10. Infographic- Mobile Search Statistics, http://icebreakerconsulting.com/infographic-mobile-search-statistics/ data accessed May 2014.

11. 30+ compelling mobile search statistics, https://econsultancy.com/blog/63230-30-compelling-mobile-search-statistics#i.s55dk5630eirpj data accessed May 2014.

12. 10 Mobile Search Statistics- Showing the Past and Predicting the Future [INFOGRAPHIC],

http://socialmediatoday.com/stuartwainstock/2031461/10-mobile-search-statistics-showing-past-and-predicting-future data accessed May 2014.

13. Building Smartphone-Optimized Websites, https://developers.google.com/webmasters/smartphone-sites/details data accessed May 2014.

Index

About Us Page, 90, 104, 105, 106, 109, 110, 180

Active Voice, 100

Adaptive Websites, 114

ALT Text, 145

Authority Symbols, 64

Auto Responder, 88

B2B Buyer, 54

B2C Buyer, 54

Best Buyer, 5, 9, 10, 18, 19, 20, 23, 25, 27, 28, 29, 37, 52, 56, 62, 84, 97, 99, 133, 149, 171, 179

Bounce Rate, 157

Branding, 39, 40, 42, 43, 44, 46, 48, 49, 85, 94, 179

Breadcrumb Navigation, 145

Broken Link Checker, 130

Broken Links, 130

Build Trust, 54, 60, 70, 86, 105, 179

Business Description, 84

Buyer Keywords, 33

Buyer Profile, 18, 25

Buyer Profiles, 10, 23, 34, 36, 37, 53, 84, 179

Buying Behavior, 54

Buying Cycle, 8

Call to Actions, 29, 61, 71, 74, 77, 79, 87, 94, 101, 122, 142, 147, 157, 170

Choice of Color, 46

Colors, 41, 42, 43, 46, 47, 49, 61, 63, 76, 77, 85, 101, 179

Competition, 22, 51, 53, 59, 71, 72, 79, 81, 82, 104, 109, 121, 142, 165, 166, 168, 176, 178, 180

Content Management System, 125

Content Writing, 87, 90, 99, 101, 139

Conversion, 13, 14, 18, 26, 52, 53, 65, 86, 154, 155, 171

Conversion Rates, 24, 157

Custom Buyer, 28

Customer Reviews, 175

Design Brief, 83, 88, 95, 96, 124, 127, 180

Design Objectives, 85

Did You Know?, 68

Domain Name, 41, 43, 45

Doug Williams Digital Marketing, 15

Drip Marketing, 55

Drip Marketing Campaign, 68

eCommerce, 78, 87, 144, 155

Education Based Marketing, 65, 66, 69

Educational Marketing, 67

Emphasized Text, 145

External Backlinks, 80

Features Buyer, 27

First Impression, 73

Free Report, 9, 54, 56, 60, 62, 68, 87, 136

Google Adwords, 155

Google Analytics, 83, 154, 157, 158, 159, 163, 164, 170, 172, 181

H1 Tags, 143, 145

Home Page, 23, 29, 51, 61, 74, 77, 90, 92, 96, 103, 106, 107, 109, 110, 127, 143, 146, 180

Interior Page, 85

Internal Links, 145

Key Performance Indicators, 17, 151, 153, 154

Keyword Plan, 174

Keyword Research, 24, 32, 34, 35, 37, 72, 179

Keyword Selection, 35

Landing Page, 85, 147

Local Search, 133

Logo, 41, 42, 43, 48, 49, 85, 147, 179

Lorem Ipsum, 94

MajesticSEO.com, 162, 164

market data, 65, 67, 68, 69

Measurable Objectives, 17

META Description, 91, 92, 139, 141, 142

Metrics, 17, 22, 123, 151, 152, 153, 154, 156, 158, 161, 162, 163, 164, 165, 167, 170, 171, 176, 177, 178, 181

Mobile Internet, 111

Mobile Search, 11, 111, 112, 183

Mobile Strategy, 111

Mobile Websites, 115, 117, 119, 180

Monthly Website Review, 166

Multiple Selling Sequences, 23, 29, 69, 92

Multiple Traffic Strategies, 25

Navigation, 24, 30, 64, 74, 77, 90, 93, 94, 98, 126, 144, 146

OpenSiteExplorer.org, 162, 164

Organic SEO, 133, 137, 149

Page Load Speed, 80, 118

Pay Per Click, 134, 146, 149

PDCA Cycle, 167

Personas, 23, 29, 30, 37, 59, 69, 179

Price Buyer, 27

Psychology of Search, 31

Pull Marketing, 7, 14

Push Marketing, 7

Quality Check, 129

Reference Websites, 73, 76, 82, 85, 179

Referring Domains, 80, 81

Reputology, 176

Responsive Websites, 116, 119

Sales Process, 9, 57, 59, 90

Search Engine Optimization, 101, 123

Search Psychology, 8

Selling Sequence, 13, 29, 57, 58, 59, 60, 69, 70, 123, 157, 170, 179

SEMrush.com, 162, 177

SEO Blogging, 173, 175

SEO Friendly, 144

SEO Page Plan, 72, 88

SEO Plan, 34, 36, 88, 91, 96, 101, 128, 138, 150, 180, 181

SEOQuake, 79, 80, 161, 164, 177

Shopping Cart Abandonment Rate, 155

Sitemap, 88, 91, 93, 96, 101, 123, 127, 138, 161, 180

Smartphones, 11, 12, 14, 113, 115

Social Media, 20, 25, 41, 68, 87, 135, 147, 148, 149, 172, 176

Social Proof, 64

Solutions Buyer, 28

Storyboarding, 9, 88

Targeted Audience, 84

Title Tag, 91, 139, 140, 141, 145, 159

Traffic Strategy, 20

Transactional Assurances, 64

Trust Logos, 64, 69, 86, 158

Value Proposition, 12, 53

Videos, 24, 63, 70, 77, 78, 87, 97, 107, 108, 127, 128, 129, 148, 157, 179

Wayback Machine, 45

Web Applications, 126

Webmaster Tools, 83, 158, 159, 160, 163, 170

Website Building Process, 121

Website Development Process, 127, 132

Website Objectives, 84

Website Project Team, 121

Website Purpose, 18, 25

Wireframe, 88, 93, 94, 95, 96, 106, 107, 123, 127, 180

Woorank.com, 162, 164

Writers Block, 105

Writing for SEO, 101

Writing for the Web, 97, 109

Writing Schedule, 106

www.ingramcontent.com/pod-product-compliance
Lightning Source LLC
Chambersburg PA
CBHW071428170526
45165CB00001B/444